THE NON-HUMAN PERSONA GUIDE

Damien Lutz

ISBN: 978-0-6453266-6-6

Cover design by Damien Lutz, using vector artwork from Vecteezy.com.

Lifecentred.design

Contents

Figures

About this Guide

The Non-Human Persona Guide is a synthesis of learnings from various designers and researchers from around the world on how to identify the animals, environments, and 'invisible humans' impacted by our designs to then create personas for them to represent their needs during design and business planning.

Who this guide is for

This guide is for industrial designers, digital designers, product owners, innovators, and business decision-makers who want to do what they can now to improve our world to help nurture the more significant changes we need that are taking too long to happen.

Why this guide was created

The use of personas to represent non-human and non-users is still new, so awareness of them is low, those who use them are few, and the way they are used varies. This is the first holistic study of how non-human/non-user personas are employed by different practitioners across different industries with the purpose of:

- Developing initial best practices from the synthesised knowledge
- Contributing to the further development and testing of non-human/non-user personas as legitimate tools
- Making discovery and experimentation with non-human/non-user personas easier
- Accelerating the transition to more regenerative and fairer local and global relationships between all people, animals, and planet

It's important to note that non-human/non-user personas have not been in use long enough to know their long-term impact, effectiveness, and unintended consequences, hence experimentation, setting metrics, and sharing back is important.

How to use this guide

For a complete introduction to non-human and non-user personas, read the guide end to end. The guide can then be used as an ongoing reference for experimentation and further projects.

Terminology

Before we dive in, let me clarify some words often used in this guide which may not be familiar to all.

- **Non-human**—A term to represent an animal or environment that is either a resource for a business ecosystem or impacted by it
- **Non-user**—A term to represent a human other than the user of a product/service who is either part of the product/lifecycle and supply chain or impacted by it
- **Actants**—'Actants' is used in this book in place of 'stakeholders' or 'actors'. The word 'stakeholders' was used in colonial times to refer to a person who drove wooden stakes into the ground to claim an area of land without any regard to, or negotiations with indigenous peoples
- **Life-centred Design**—A new design framework that expands human centred design from focusing on only business and user needs to also consider impacts to present, past, and future people, animals, and environments impacted by the business ecosystem
- **Business ecosystem**—A business, its products and services and their lifecycles, staff, customers, supply chain workers and partners, and other business partners (marketing, etc.)
- **Product lifecycle**—The true lifecycle of a product starts from when its materials are extracted from nature, processed into parts and products, and shipped through the supply chain, to when they are used/owned by customers, and finally to when they reused, refurbished, resold, recycled, or are discarded as waste
- **The Circular Economy and Circular Design**—The Circular Economy is an alternate economic model to today's *take-make-waste* model that depletes and pollutes natural resources and harms people. Circular Design is a way of designing with a more efficient use of materials and energy to reduce the extraction of raw materials, pollution, and waste
- **Regeneration**—While sustainable design aims to ensure there is enough resources for each season, regenerative design is about constantly reducing impacts, improving circularity, and giving back more to the environmental and human ecosystems than we take from to ensure they stay healthy, resilient, and thriving.

Online resources

This guide is accompanied by a 'virtual Journey Backpack' of tools for the methods and resources for inspiration, available at *https://lifecentred.design* where you can create a free account to access.

The tools and resources are free to use as open source to encourage experimentation and contribution to the evolution of non-human/non-user personas. Enjoy!

For any feedback or suggestions on the material in this guide or the backpack, feel free to email me at info@lifecentred.design.

Part 1

\-

The purpose
of a tree

What is the purpose of a tree?

A human's first instinct to reply to this question might be 'to make oxygen' for us to breathe.

But, of course, we know the purpose of a tree can be understood from various perspectives, as trees serve multiple important roles in the natural world as well those that benefit humans.

To create the oxygen many lifeforms breath, trees absorb carbon dioxide from the atmosphere which has helped stabilise the earth's temperature. Their complex structure also provides nesting sites, shelter, and food for birds, insects, and other creatures, contributing to the overall biodiversity of an area.

Underground, their root systems help stabilize the soil, reduce runoff, and improve water infiltration, which aids in maintaining healthy soil conditions for plant growth and preventing soil erosion.

Trees also play a role in regulating the water cycle. Their roots help absorb excess water from the ground, reducing the risk of flooding. They also release moisture into the air through a process called transpiration, which influences local humidity levels and can contribute to the formation of clouds and rainfall.

For humans, trees provide food and medicine, timber for shelter, and they contribute to tourism and recreation, attracting visitors to parks, forests, and natural landscapes, and improving the quality of life for communities.

While they are an ecosystem unto themselves, trees make no waste or pollution. What they do 'release' is used by other systems—oxygen and fruit give life to humans and other lifeforms, and even dropped and dying leaves enrich the soil and feed more lifeforms.

Everything a tree is connected to, it contributes to, and in this way, it keeps energy and matter moving. And it's powered by the safe and renewable energy of the sun.

It's important to recognize that these purposes of trees are interconnected and interdependent, and the conservation and sustainable management of trees and forests are crucial to the well-being of our planet and future generations.

But it's not only trees that are designed with this interconnected, waste- and pollution-free lifecycle—all life, including us humans, are designed with this symbiotic lifecycle, from the materials we are made from, to what happens to those materials when we die.

Now, imagine if everything humans created, from our homes to our furniture to our utensils and our technology, were designed to work like trees.

Everything we make is already an ecosystem—unfortunately, many of our creations, such as disposable products, are unhealthy ones for the planet that either block the flow of energy by locking it up in non-biodegradable waste, or reconfigure matter into toxic 'anti-life' waste materials.

When viewing products as part of a lifecycle system, we can no longer deny responsibility for releasing something into the living world as a new ecosystem of materials, people, and energy spanning the time and distance far beyond the target-user's use of the product, and which can exist long after the producer stops producing and collecting profits.

Decades of designing without this regard for environmental and social impact, combined with the rapid expansion of consumers, has far overextended humanity's limits of operation and fuelled the intensity of the climate crisis and widespread inequality.

I'm sure you're aware of these problems, so what I want to ask is:

How can you design your product to be more like a tree?

Or your service, or your business?

Should we think of a chair and its lifecycle as if it were a separated branch falling slowly over time, made of waste, and destined to decompose and give back to nature?

Do we change our perspectives of a business and product lifecycle to view them not just as sources of profit and livelihoods, but also as funnels for energy, so that we may identify and untangle the blockages, to redesign them for greater interconnectedness that nourishes not just itself but the environments, animals, and the invisible humans connected to them?

To make things more like trees, we need to evolve human-centred design to consider all life, to become *life-centred*.

Life-centred design expands human-centred design to consider the impacts on the planet and all the people impacted by the business ecosystem.

One method to expand design to be more than human-centred is to recognise all life as key actants through the use of personas.

14

Non-human and non-user personas

If you're in product design or marketing, you'll be familiar with 'user personas'—fictional character documents, based on interviews and contextual enquiry with real customers, that summarise different types of customers with similar needs.

Just like personas for human target users, non-human and non-user personas enable designers and decision-makers to keep the needs of these actants in mind *as they make design and business decisions* to reduce their impact upon non-humans/non-users, and ultimately to regenerate them. This empathy keeps a non-human/non-user's well-being at the front of our minds, so that we see them not just as a resource but as a fellow actant to respect.

But personas are not just a decision-making tool.

They are also a process which educates the creators and establishes a shared understanding in a team and business, so that as we research to create a persona for, say, a tree, we learn about that tree, we understand it more and its importance as an organic machine keeping energy and matter flowing through the earth's liveable habitat, creating that habitat on which we depend.

This immersive process establishes our empathy for the non-human/non-users, and the tool helps us perpetuate our empathy.

With this renewed respect for nature, we can also emulate its sustainable and regenerative forms and functions, to slowly infuse these into our creations, so that they too become interconnected and free of waste and pollution... just like a tree.

This empathy, this connection of emotion and awareness generated by the non-human/non-user persona process and tool could be the tendrils of robust roots reconnecting modern designers, businesses, and citizens to nature's cycles long respected by older cultures.

That is the dream behind non-human/non-user personas, but they are new versions of old imperfect tools, so we need to experiment hard and cautiously, and share back generously.

This book aims to accelerate this experimentation and enrich our use and evolution of non-human and non-user personas, so that we respect and protect all life to ensure it thrives well into the future.

Some would argue we need to create less and live simpler. I agree. But I also believe that such a drastic change won't happen soon without government action to mobilise the many. Or perhaps the effects of climate change will compound faster than we ever dared to imagine and force those drastic changes.

NON HUMAN PERSONA

Trees

> We provide oxygen and limit carbon in the atmosphere. We reduce air pollution, provide food and shelter for wildlife, minimise erosion and maintain healthy soil, increase rainfall, and absorb sunlight as energy. We communicate and collaborate together. We are essential for life on Earth, up to 15 billion/year, reducing our forests by over 80 million hectares since 1990. Urbanisation and climate change threaten us with increased wildfires, invasive species, and habitat degradation making it harder for us to bounce back.

❯ Material extraction ☐ Supply chain ☐ Sales channels ❯ Product in use ❯ 2nd life ❯ Waste

NEEDS

Reduced deforestation

Time to grow

Healthy soil

_____

_____

CHALLENGES

Deforestation

Urbanisation

Climate change

Increased wildfires

~~Invasive species~~

Habitat degradation

PROTECTION

PREVENTION	HEALING
Use less paper	Plant a tree
Recycle paper and cardboard	Practice eco-forestry
Use recycled products	Raise awareness
Buy only sustainable wood products	Respect the rights of indigenous people
~~Don't buy products containing palm oil~~	~~Support organisation fighting deforestation~~
~~Reduce meat consumption~~	
Respect the rights of indigenous ~~people~~	

Non-Human Environment Persona, Damian Lutz 2022. http://lifecentred.design, NonCommercial 4.0 International (CC BY-NC 4.0)

Figure 1 - A persona for Trees

Until more significant changes happen, I believe we can choose to do what we can with what influence and power we have. Just as the many forces impacting the stability of the planet's thin sliver of space for life seem to be compounding, there must also be positive tipping points of change, possibly activated by millions of individuals doing what they can at the ground level.

However, the impacts on those who create and use non-human/non-user personas also have the potential for evolving the use of non-human/non-user personas beyond design:

- Reconnecting with our planet
- Shifting from passively hoping for change to *actively manifesting* change

These impacts could evolve education, business culture, and local and global discussions to create the more significant changes life on Earth needs, such as further enshrining the rights of nature in all constitutions.

As I created personas for trees, bees, e-waste, child labourers, and others, many emotions arose—creating personas can be confronting, because the process reconnects us with our impact on the world by making us see and feel these impacts, empathising with those impacted, and reminding us that our relationship could be a lot healthier.

But the process also shows us *how* we can make things healthier. This can foster a personal shift from passive hope to active hope through learning the skills and mindsets to respond to today's wicked problems in tangible, practical, and measurable ways.

Creating and using personas can be a very emotive, sometimes traumatic, and yet a very inspiring experience—a journey that many present and future humans and other lifeforms could greatly benefit from.

Designing for more than human business and users

Respecting the thriving existence of non-humans has roots in First Nations People's animistic beliefs and practices.

Animism is the belief that all things—non-human entities like natural objects, plants, animals, spirit beings, and the weather—possess an individual spirit.

Practising animism could include assigning yourself and others a 'totem', which represented the non-human entities and which you must learn about, and care and advocate for. In this way, totems (an anglicisation of the Ojibwe word for clan, 'doodem') were used to respect and connect with the non-human world.

17

For example, in First Nations Australian totemism, people belonging to the Emu as a totem must learn and teach others about Emu needs and how to respect them, and they are held accountable for what happens to the Emu.

Lost to the developing world over centuries, respect for the rights for animals re-emerged through the controversial idea of legal personhood for animals. There has also been much research into designing with animals in mind—including designing technology for animals to interact with—by great designers and scholars, such as Steve North, Hanna Wirman, Anne Galloway, Patricia Pons, and Donna Haraway. Their research has fed into the evolution of interspecies design, which produced interactive experiences for animals such as:

- A touch-screen for a gorilla to learn language and communicate
- Underwater keyboards for dolphins
- An automatic robotic milking system for dairy cows to voluntarily milk themselves
- Buttons for dogs to open doors for disabled humans
- A video device with a paw interface allowing pets to 'call' their owners

Animals found their way into design personas in the design of sustainable food systems in 2014.

And in 2020, anthropologist and UX researcher Monika Sznel published her environment-centred design articles in which she proposed environmental personas for UX, service, and product design, along with an 'actant map' to identify non-humans/non-users.

Note: The totem information in this book was sourced from information written by First Nations peoples.

Life-centred personas

Sznel's work inspired exploration by other designers, such as the persona tools designed by myself, and persona implementation explored by Jeroen Spoelstra, founder of The Life-centred Design School. Interaction professor and author Martin Tomitsch formally argued the case for non-human personas in his research paper 'Non-Human Personas: Including Nature in the Participatory Design of Smart Cities' which introduced a hypothetical framework based on academic research and experimentation.

Sznel argued that non-human personas differ from user personas in that non-human personas should be primarily based on facts, sourced from respectable global organisations like the UN, more localised affiliate-free organisations and experts, scientists, and the people impacted by any environmental concerns relevant to the product.

However, their purpose is the same as a human user persona—to enable designers and decision-makers to empathise with non-human and non-user needs. They should be written in a way that conveys the non-human as a living, vulnerable, powerful entity to be heard and respected.

Combining Nielson Norman Group's user persona and Sznel's non-human persona guidance, the purpose of a non-human persona could be defined as '*A realistic and fact-based representation of non-human entities to ensure their inclusion in all stages of design and design-making by fostering human empathy, awareness, and respect*'.

Non-human personas are evolving in other disciplines and mediums, too.

An extended reality agency, BlackRhino VR, created an evocative non-human persona video of the largest dumpsite in Eastern Africa.

Blackrhinovr Persona

Creating and using personas of non-human stakeholders can help product engineers and digital designers think systemically about their designs' impact on non-users, animals, and environments along the lifecycle of a product, at the digital experience, and from the individual and community to global levels—and over time.

What is a non-human?

Non-humans are the planetary elements, environments, animals, and entities often considered 'non-living'.

Animals might include:
- Animals of all sizes (amphibians, reptiles, birds, and mammals) to insects and microbes
- Animals on land, sea, in the air, and underground

- Domestic, livestock, captive, or wild
- Whether 'proven' sentient or not

Planetary elements and environments:

- Vegetation (e.g., trees, forests, swamps, etc.)
- Water systems (oceans, lakes, rivers, freshwater)
- Climate and weather systems
- Air, soil, landforms (e.g., mountains, hills, etc.)
- Sunlight, noise, temperature
- Microbes, viruses, diseases
- Ecosystems of the above, and biodiversity as a whole

Actants often considered 'non-living':

- Data
- E-waste
- Dumping grounds
- Abandoned dwellings
- The Great Garbage Patch in the North Pacific Ocean

Non-human personas, however, only represent two of the life-centred design actant groups—animals and environments.

More than user

The third actant group, 'non-users', represents the 'invisible' humans directly or indirectly impacted by a product and business ecosystem at any phase of the product lifecycle, which could include:

- Individuals, communities, and employees of organisations *working within* the product lifecycle
- Individuals and communities *not directly involved* in the lifecycle but who are impacted by it, such as local communities, indigenous people, the homeless, etc.
- We can also include different human knowledge systems, ways of existing, and belief systems as a non-user to create personas for

Non-user personas may represent a real person or a persona group. They may be a combination of fictional representation and scientific data.

Together, non-human and non-user personas help designers and decision-makers identify and respect life-centred design's three actant groups—all people, lifeforms, and environments.

Types of personas and their uses

Specific personas

When specific non-humans/non-users are identified (e.g., a specie, group, or individual animal or plant), personas can be created for them to ensure their needs are respected and to seek ways for the business to become a caretaker for them. Specific personas are good for focusing on how a product and business can do *specifically* to reduce impact and nurture that non-human/non-user. If your purpose is to innovate the entire product/business, specific personas can be used as complimentary lenses to a broader life-centred redesign.

Generalised personas

Personas can also be created that generalise 'life' and its habitat, Earth.

For example:

- A 'Nature' persona can represent all lifeforms (environments and animals)
- An 'Invisible Humans' persona could represent all the non-users to look for (factory workers, local communities, indigenous)

Being so generalised, these personas can generate broad ideas for innovation at all stages and levels, from product to lifecycle to the wider business ecosystem. This makes generalised personas an excellent warm up exercise to identify a broad range of impacts and opportunities for circular, inclusive, and regenerative innovation before applying a deeper analysis, and to introduce clients, students, participants, etc. to life-centred thinking.

See examples of persona types in the **Persona Library** at *lifecentred.design*.

When to create non-human/non-user personas

Creating personas is about designing for needs. Sometimes non-humans/non-users and their key needs are clear enough without the need for creating personas.

Also, creating them with accuracy can be time-consuming.

However, as mentioned earlier, personas are as important as a process to experience as they are a tool to use. That experience deepens a designer's connection with the non-humans/non-users and uncovers what they didn't know they didn't know.

Consider the reach of your product, service, or business—the greater it is, the more important it is to life-centre its design and ecosystem, and the more important it is to ensure the accuracy and depth of understanding the impacted non-human/non-users.

Also consider your relationship with the non-human/non-users—the closer and longer that relationship, the more important to understand and respect them.

Then there are factors to consider beyond your product and business, such as the non-humans/non-users' importance to keeping life on Earth stable and balanced, whether locally or globally, and the health of their own existence.

Again, it can be hard to know these considerations without doing the research that creates personas.

Challenges and limitations

Since non-human/non-user personas have only been in use for a short while, and with some regeneration projects such as planting new forests taking years to show their positive impact, there is not enough evidence yet to measure and validate their effects.

Also, non-human/non-user personas can have the same limitations as human personas, such as:

- Lack of accuracy and completeness
- Being made with biased images and content
- Harmful stereotyping
- Generalisation leaving out the marginalised
- Not being kept updated
- Not referred to often (weakening empathy)

Any of the above can cause unintended rebound effects that might negate the positive effects and/or worsen the situation. Hence, fact-based data and expert input are important. If experts can't be interviewed and/or included, applying best research practices will help ensure research is accurate (see the **Research Guide**).

While using non-human/non-user personas to design products and business 'to be more like trees' seems to have only positive impacts, the modern design world thought the same about human-centred design when it first evolved, while we completely missed or ignored the impacts to the rest of the planet. So, let's stay vigilant and critical of these tools.

Part 2

-

Personas
in practice

Introduction

To research the different ways non-human/non-user personas could be used to inform design decisions so that they respect non-human and non-user needs, I interviewed digital and service designers who had used them from Germany, Spain, UK, and the US. I also analysed detailed academic and business projects and included insight from my own projects.

Interviews

I discussed the use of non-human/non-user personas in:

- **Service design** with Victor Udoewa, US
- **Community and business design** with Jeroen Spoelstra, *Unbeaten Studio and The Life-centred Design School*, Spain
- **Web and mobile design** with Sandy Daehnert, *Green The Web*, Germany
- **Introducing non-human personas** to clients with Fiona Tout and Ben Serbutt, &us, UK

Analysis

I analysed the following published work and experimentation with non-human/non-user personas, including one of my own early experiments:

- **Persona creation, UX and service design** by Monika Sznel, Poland
- **Urban digital interface design** by Martin Tomitsch, with Joel Fredericks, Dan Vo, Jessica Frawley, Marcus Foth, Australia
- **App interface design** by Isabella Bain and Martin Tomitsch, Australia
- **UX** design by Damien Lutz, Australia

Key areas of investigation

When synthesising the research insights, common themes emerged which later informed the method's structure:

- Identifying and selecting non-humans/non-users
- Creating personas
- How personas were used to inform design decisions and examples
- Frequency of use
- Other uses
- General insights to inform principles

UX and service design (Poland)

Monika Sznel

UX and Service Designer

This insight is from an analysis of "Your next persona will be non-human—tools for environment-centred designers"—Medium, 2020

As mentioned earlier, Monika Sznel is a design anthropologist, UX researcher, and service designer who is also passionate about environment-centred design.

Sznel wrote about environment-centred design in 2020, sharing her **Actant Mapping Canvas** and **Non-human Persona** tools.

These two tools—a business ecosystem map of the impacted actants beyond humans, and personas representing these actants—remain the core of life-centred design today.

Sznel was also part of the Good Girl gang who designed a hypothetical UX for Uber Eats project, for an ecological hackathon in Warsaw in September 2019, to encourage a plant-based diet.

Below are insights from analysing Sznel's published work.

Identifying non-humans/non-users

1. Define a life-centred challenge/problem of your product/business
2. Use the **Actant Mapping Canvas** to map direct humans and non-humans actants directly impacted by the challenge or problem
3. Map indirect actants using systems thinking and scientific resources, such as Doughnut economics, the Ellen Macarthur website for circular thinking, etc.
4. Map the causes and effects on actants
5. Use 'What if?' questions to explore future impacts (e.g., 'What happens if we use this resource for X years?')

Creating personas

Monika argued that non-human personas are different to human personas as they should be based on data and facts since they cannot speak for themselves. This can be achieved by:

- Co-creating personas with colleagues
- Conduct primary research (e.g., interview experts, representatives of NGOs working in the environmental sector, scientists with expertise in a field, internal employees, or coolheaded and fact-based activists, etc.) to validate secondary analysis (e.g., statistics, data, and reports delivered by the UN or other respectable organizations with no political/economic affiliations, internal data gathered by your company, etc.)
- Summarise with fact-based stories
- Be believable and convincing

Using personas

Aim to innovate without compromising business goals:

- Gain insights from the actant mapping about the damage caused
- Brainstorm solutions using the value of business
- Explore how UX can support these
- Share early internally for ideas (e.g., run an internal survey to ask *How Might We?* to address the needs and challenges)

Examples of personas informing design decisions

Using nature as an actant for the Uber Eats innovation, Monika and the Good Girl Gang employed the following UX strategies to promote to users the choice of plant-based meals:

- *Prioritising* the promotion of plant-based products
- Improving vegan *filters*
- Allowing users to create favourite plant-based *lists*
- *Balancing actant and business needs* to respect the actant while not compromising business goals

Other uses

Monika recommends using the personas also as a tool to influence business and actants to become more sustainably-minded:

- Take personas to product feature demonstrations
- Share personas with colleagues (but don't impose personas upon them)
- Share with allies to create broader connections (e.g., Climate Designers, Client Earth, Earth Justice, etc.)

Monika also argued personas could be created for non-humans identified as threats, such as the COVID19 virus.

Monika best sums up her use of non-human personas with these words:

"It's an optimistic action driven by data and coolheaded analysis."

Community and business design (Spain)

Jeroen Spoelstra

Product and Service Designer | Unbeaten Studio

Interviewed 2022

Jeroen Spoelstra, UX designer and co-founder of The Life-centred Design School in Spain, has been exploring and applying life-centred design through a process that focuses on immersing designers and participants in natural environments.

Using 'a combination of emotional narrative and scientific research', his persona approach aims to create an emotional connection between designers and the natural habitats to generate a feeling of responsibility.

Below are insights from an interview with Jeroen Spoelstra in 2022.

Project 1—Tourism design

Non-human actants: Ibón de Plan (a snow and ice lake in Spain)

Identifying non-humans/non-users

Concerned about the impacts of tourists mountain-bike riding around a lake near his home, Jeroen gathered local people and visiting students to explore the idea of creating a persona for the lake.

Creating personas

1. *Gather the team*—Jeroen gathered representatives from the townhall and the mountain bike centre, a Film maker, and five design students
2. *Map the system*—The group made a context map of the lake's tourism ecosystem, defining actant groups such as impacted species, resources, etc.
3. *Connect with nature*—The group explored the lake region by walking in silence from the wilderness to the tourism areas as an immersive means of connecting with the environment
4. *Collect insights*—The group collected insights to start creating a persona and identify what else needed to be researched
5. *Research*—The group then researched for scientific data about the lake

6. *Explore unintended consequences*—Using the Impact Ripple Canvas, the group explored unintended impacts of tourism activities on the lake region ecosystem

Persona formats

Spoelstra's group compiled their insights into two artefacts which were collated on a web page:

- An essay, talking about the environmental and social purpose of the lake and its history, challenges, relationship with humanity, and opportunities for the relationship to improve
- An audio file, spoken in the first person as if the lake spoke itself

Spoelstra noted that hearing the audio file was a key moment of empathy for many participants and audiences, as it connected them emotionally to an impression of the lake's predicament. He noted also that there was a variety of formats to choose from, such as images, video, audio, infographics, a theatre play, posters, a website, an article, visual stories, or combinations.

From this, Spoelstra says the non-human persona is just a tool to collect data. The real impact comes from how the persona is communicated to amplify the emotional connection with the reader—the format depends on its purpose and audience.

Using personas

Spoelstra plans to work further with the town to determine actions from the persona work.

Project 2—Business and product design

Non-human actants: The local environment

Identifying non-humans/non-users

A furniture business in Norway looking to design an eco-friendly furniture service system contacted Spoelstra for help with a life-centred approach.

Spoelstra looked first at what local resources could be used by researching the local environment to understand regional elements like the soil and local spruce pines.

Working remotely from Spain, he used online resources such as the 'Global Safety Net' which advised what is needed for regeneration in critical regions around the world.

Spoelstra combined this research into a general description of the area to guide life-centred design making.

> "We learnt soil is good to capture carbon,
> maybe better than trees, but soil needs trees...
> It's a game you're constantly playing."

Selecting non-humans/non-users

At first, Spoelstra was looking at using native Norway spruce, but after discussion with the client they decided using an invasive spruce so the native one could regenerate.

He also determined a non-user—a regenerative farmer.

Using personas

Spoelstra then connected the non-human and non-user insights with the business by designing how the farmer and eco-business could work together.

Frequency of use: Used at all stages of the process, from discovery to design

Spoelstra used the persona often throughout the process to identify potential problems and systemic challenges (e.g., carbon accounting, overconsumption, etc.) which very much engaged the client's interest in the approach.

Examples of non-human personas informing design decisions

- *Product material choice*—As mentioned above, Spoelstra choose the invasive spruce as the furniture material because that would be better for the local environment
- *Payment model design*—Spoelstra explored the idea of customers paying a subscription which could be reinvested into carbon capture and local environmental efforts
- *Regenerative commitments*—Spoelstra also explored the idea of using profits to regenerate the land that becomes barren once all the invasive specie had been used

Limitations

- *Time to see benefits*—long term projects like replanting trees takes time to see the benefits

Other uses

Spoelstra advises personas can also be used as:

- A metric tool when a second 'future' version of the persona is made to compare with the first persona to assess the impact of the design decisions
- A tool for creating public awareness
- A tool for inspiring change in companies and governments

Social and system-level service design (US)

Victor Udoewa

Social and system level service designer | US Federal Government, NASA

Interviewed 2022

Victor Udoewa is a service and experience design lead who has worked with the needs of non-humans such as plants, terrains, ice, water, and air for projects with the US Federal Government, NASA, and local communities.

When it comes to non-humans, Udoewa also includes 'non-living' things, such as buildings. He draws this thinking from the indigenous wisdom that recognises there is sentience in rocks, mountains, etc., and that the living/non-living separation does not exist.

Udoewa is also a great implementer of, and advocate for Radical Participatory Design (RPD) which he teaches on the Interaction Design Foundation platform (IXDF).

Udoewa's approach gathers people who can bring different types of knowledge to the project—intuitive, embodied, aesthetic, community, relational, spiritual, and lived experiential knowledge—to avoid mainstream and institutionalised design knowledge dominating the design process. Udoewa includes these knowledge bearers as full-fledged members of the design and research team, so their values, ways of being, knowledge, and ways of designing lead the process, and so they also own the produced solutions and artefacts.

These knowledge bearers can include people at the bottom of social hierarchies, as they tend to have a more accurate understanding of the impacts of damaged or unhealthy creations due to them being in direct contact with the negative externalities of people of power who are insulating themselves from the effect.

Udoewa argues technologists and innovation specialists have been using non-human needs for a long time, such as defining the temperature requirements for a computer server. But, with the rise of Human-centred Design, modern design became so focused on human needs and perspectives that it forgot to employ a more holistic understanding of the interconnections between humans and the rest of creation.

Identifying non-humans/non-users

Working at the service level, Udoewa uses systems thinking to identify the boundary of the system of the project and its influence, which in turn reveals the non-humans/non-users:

1. Frame the system with knowledge bearers
2. Set the boundaries of what will be considered by the project, recognising that resources, influences, and forces move in and out of the boundaries of the system
3. Consider the non-human/non-user needs within the boundaries of the system

Through his participatory approach, the process of identifying non-humans "comes out of and from the community" which is represented by the gathered knowledge bearers, who are also closer and more connected to the ways in which harm to non-humans affects the community.

"The identification of non-humans, non-human needs come from the community."

Selecting non-humans/non-users

Determining which non-humans to focus on can be done by considering which non-human/non-users are:

- The most vulnerable
- The most affected
- At key leverage points in the system where a particular effort or intervention will have the most impact

Creating personas

Udoewa works more with behavioural archetypes and 'characters' rather than personas. Characters are based on three criteria:

- Anxieties and motivations
- Goal progress events—Events that move the human or non-human along the pathway from awareness to interest to desire to action

- Goal progress situations—Situations in which the human/non-human must make decisions or is forced to make a decision about whether they will take the action or not to complete the goal

A project can also consider what the non-humans/non-users tell us directly (e.g., how they engage with us and the environment), and indirectly (e.g., how the environment impacts them).

But regardless of whether personas or characters are used, for Udoewa, it's the process of learning about non-humans/non-users that creates a shared understanding.

What information to collect

The data to collect is generally determined by the needs of the non-humans/non-users, and by the process. For example, if defining a future vision of a subject, Udoewa will include more than *needs*, but also strengths and assets for flourishment. Udoewa also looks for common needs across the community and the non-human to focus on.

> *"If a human need is equitable drinking water, what is the natural source of that water, and the terrain or structures that the water flows through, and the impact of these flows, such as carving out canyons, valleys, and mountains, bringing salts that are in the air, rain, and ocean to the shore?"*

How to gather information

- Study the non-human/non-user in their environment
- Note what the non-human/non-user tell us directly and/or indirectly
- Search historical data about the non-humans/non-users and the project's environment (e.g., look at the rings of a tree from a hundred years ago, examine various layers of rock, etc.)
- Consider variables of the non-human (e.g., the needs of a new building would be different from the needs of an old building)

Persona format

Udoewa doesn't use just one particular format.

He might use something as simple as a list of needs in a document or on a board. He may also use any research output that is suitable—a system map, value proposition canvas, ecosystem map, journey map of a resource, journey map of the non-human/non-user through history, asset statements or map, environmental assessments, equity assessments, problem statements, etc.

Using personas

Frequency of use: Used at all stages of the process, from discovery to design

Udoewa uses non-human insights often throughout the design process, referring to their needs whenever he would refer to the human user needs.

Udoewa also updates personas as needed during the process and over time.

"I'm always referring back to the needs, that's what we're trying to satisfy."

Assessing design

1. Assess the needs, use the same steps when making sure that human needs are represented
2. Ask yourself questions:
   - For the human problem we solve, are you creating that problem for the non-human?
   - What are common needs across humans and non-humans?
   - Will the design now or in the future violate or detract from the needs of non-humans?
3. Consider the energy used, any waste or pollution, and heat generated
4. Consider digital services as tangible products somewhere—what's the hardware of any software or UX, and how does that impact non-humans?

While Udoewa works at the service, social, and systems level, he says his character work does also inform products requiring digital applications.

While he argues digital experiences can't really meet non-human needs directly as they are not usually about non-human interaction, the non-human needs and values defined at the systems or social level can flow through the process and give direction to the digital designer, who can ensure the product and UX carry those same values by:

- Helping the human users interact with software in ways that uplift and support the needs of all creation
- Helping the human users learn what actions through the software, and outside the software, can support the flourishing of all creation

Udoewa suggests digital designers can use non-human/non-user personas by asking themselves questions such as:

- Is the user behaviour negatively affecting non-humans?
- How can the design inform the users about the non-humans and non-human needs?

Project—Adapting the experience of a learning service

Non-human actants: Air

Udoewa worked on a digital literacy service project in India, which also involved UX, UI, content strategy, information architecture, visual design, business design, communications design, organization design, and learning design.

The project involved getting information to groups of people in different areas to train them on a software.

Identifying non-humans/non-users

The 'air' became a non-human actant for the project, as the team didn't want their activities to produce any air pollution which was already a serious problem in the area.

Examples of personas informing design decisions

- *Modes of transport that reduce impact*—To reducing overall energy use and pollution output, the team changed the experience of the educational service by delivering it through a bike program instead of sending out the many facilitators to the many different locations in individual vehicles.

The facilitators rode out to areas on bikes with devices and internet hot spots to provide training in various villages across India.

- *Distributing a service*—For delivering the same project in Bangladesh, Udoewa choose a mobile option instead of a stationary service using buses to deliver the service, so that just the service used energy and caused pollution instead of thousands of people. This mobile option also brought internet access to many 'non-users' of the project who they met along the way, and by using the same bus route each time, local animals had the chance to adapt to the buses regular passing.

Limitations

Udoewa highlighted that non-human/non-user personas have the same limitations as user personas in that they:

- Are often used once to infuse empathy but then get abandoned
- Can be extraneous in irrelevant detail that implicitly is interpreted as important or infused with bias
- Often don't represent the already marginalised due to their summarising nature
- Date quickly and are not updated often enough, if at all, due to lack of a plan for maintaining and no understanding of the signals for when to update them

Other uses

- **To influence**—Start embedding the use of non-human needs in the process as a way of saying to business and actants 'We're not going to be human-centred design, we're going to be life-centred'
- **'Insights crashing'**—An activity Udoewa uses after research to tie brainstorming to specific research outputs:
    - Put all the needs up on a board
    - Add all the user insights, including experiential insights, market research, futures research insights, system insights, quantitative data, etc.
    - Select a few insights (e.g., customer insight + non-human need + user quote + data research point, etc.)
    - Brainstorm the combined impact of these insights

- **Future visions**—For creating a future vision, focus on desires rather than just needs, and what makes the non-human/non-user *thrive*
- **Design principles**—Synthesise the persona needs into design principles that can also inform product and digital design

Digital product design (Germany)

Sandy Daehnert

Sustainable UX/UI Designer | greentheweb.com

Interviewed 2022

Sandy Daehnert is a UX/UI designer based in Germany who founded www.greentheweb.com in 2019 from which she generously shares her experiences, knowledge, tools, and resources for ecological and social sustainable digital design.

Daehnert has created and used personas for various non-humans such as *Nature, Cologne as a city, The Atlantic Ocean*, and the *Thuringian Forest* in Germany.

Daehnert uses non-human personas to:

- Make more ecological and sustainable UX/UI choices
- Determine what's important to talk about in digital products in terms of sustainability to bring more intention and purpose into the project
- Reaffirm to actants how important sustainable UX/UI is and to ensure the process keeps that in focus

Daehnert generally creates her personas as documents before the design process begins, and then refers to them often throughout the research, design, iteration, implementation, and post-launch analysis stages.

> *"...find out what's important to talk about in the digital products in terms of sustainability. To bring more intention and purpose into the project."*

Empathising

Daehnert suggests connecting with nature at the start of design using an imagination exercise to consider the non-human's needs, desires, and their relationship with humanity (what they give and take from each other).

Identifying non-humans/non-users

Explore which non-humans/non-users are directly and indirectly impacted by the project's ecosystem and note them all.

Selecting non-humans/non-users

Choose specific non-humans to work with by considering:

- Which are most directly impacted by the project?
- Which are negatively impacted?
- Which can be positively impacted?

Creating Personas

Research

- Go to the environment of the non-human to *feel* their experience
- Perform secondary research to gather insights about the true state of the non-human
- Use verified data to avoid perpetuating stereotypes
- Note also what data can be used to measure the impacts of using the non-human persona

Hypothesise

Combine key information into a persona document and make hypotheses about their needs and desires, etc.

- Name
- Age
- Quote
- Health
- Lifestyle and Job
- Needs and Problems
- Values
- Desires, wishes, and dreams

Pause and validate

Leave the persona for a few days and then conduct further research to validate your assumptions by performing primary research such as talking to experts.

Engage the team/business

Share the persona with the wider team and business and ask for feedback and input on how it may be used to start shifting the human-centric perspective to an environment-wide one. Product and business ideas can come from this stage, too, says Daehnert, as the wider business thinks about its responsibilities, such as making packaging, materials, banking, partnerships, web hosting, development processes, and workflows more ecological.

Also, personas can be used to encourage the business to use them beyond the design process, such as in marketing and business decision meetings.

Using Personas

Frequency of use: Used at all stages of the process, from discovery to design and post-launch analysis.

Empathise

Connect with the non-human again using an imagination exercise to empathise.

Assessing design

Review the design and ask yourself questions about how the persona's needs, desires, etc, are impacted by the design.

- How is the persona negatively impacted and how can this be reduced?
- How are they positively impacted and how can this be enhanced?
- What else can be done to nurture the non-human?

Examples of non-human persons informing design decisions

- *Web copy*—In a project where Daehnert created a persona for the city of Cologne, the persona influenced how the digital product was communicated, deepening the conversation and intent on the website
- *UI design*—Daehnert integrated donation options in an online shop for projects supporting the non-human

Limitations

Daehnert recognises non-human/non-user personas are not comprehensive, and she warns strongly about the accidental embedding of stereotypes and the designer's own bias into non-human personas. However, she argues, they are still an effective tool for empathy.

Other insight

Daehnert also advocates for ensuring the personas are allowed to change and grow over time, as designers and business learn more about the non-humans.

Urban digital interface design (Australia)

Martin Tomitsch

Head of the Transdisciplinary School at University of Technology Sydney

With **Joel Fredericks, Dan Vo, Jessica Frawley**, and **Marcus Foth**

This insight is from an analysis of "Non-Human Personas: Including Nature in the Participatory Design of Smart Cities"—Journal of Interaction Design & Architecture(s), 2021

Exploring how non-human personas could be used as a means of including nature in the design of smart cities, the following three projects were collated by Martin Tomitsch into a research article for the Interaction Design and Architecture Journal:

1. Smart urban furniture
2. The external interface of an autonomous vehicle
3. A visualised data interface capturing citizen opinion

The first project allowed for experimentation with non-human personas and informed the development of a non-human persona framework, which was then applied hypothetically to projects 2 and 3.

Project 1—Smart urban furniture

Non-human actants: Possums, plants, birds, bees

As an educational assignment, this conceptual project aimed to explore how smart urban furniture could be designed in a way that allowed for the harmonious cohabitation of humans with natural ecosystems. Based on how a park bench might be designed with the consideration of non-humans, this project was unique in that it explored a design that both humans and non-humans would interact with.

Identifying and selecting non-humans/non-users

Focusing on native species local to the area of the installed furniture, the designers defined possums as the primary non-human.

They then determined several plants as secondary non-humans which provided sources of food and nesting materials for the possums. A twiner plant was also identified as providing climbing access for possums, which then led to the selection of two bird species.

Creating personas

A persona document for 'Beans, the possum' was created, including a photo, backstory, motivations, frustrations, and habitat issues.

Using Personas

Frequency of use: Used throughout the conceptualisation process

Examples of non-human personas informing design decisions:

- *Removing product features*—Considering the well-being of birds, wireless charging stations were removed from the design
- *Adding features*—To provide a water source for possums, bees, birds, and irrigation for the plants, a rainwater system was added
- *Adapting features*—To reduce the impact on possums, birds, and bees at night, sensors were adapted to activate lights that provided visibility and safety for humans on their approach and deactivating when not needed

Limitations

- Lack of accuracy and completeness of research
- Risk of being biased by the designer's mindset, which could lead to design decisions that negatively interfere with the species and their ecosystem
- Risk for biased personas being used by designers to justify decisions

To address these limitations, the study proposed adding a step to the non-human process that created a collation of experts to assist in capturing insight about the non-humans so that the personas could speak more scientifically on their behalf.

A proposed non-human persona framework

1. Identify the non-humans/non-users

- Identify primary non-humans—Consider those that are most common, most at risk, and/or most relevant to humanity (e.g., companion animals, livestock, etc.)
- Identify secondary non-humans—Those supporting the primary (e.g., as a co-dependent specie, as food, etc.)
- Explore unintended impacts, using tools such as the Impact Ripple Canvas
- Be iterative—Throughout the design process, the classification of primary and secondary actants may change based on new learnings or input from experts

2. Creating personas

Persona formats

A 1-2 page document.

Process

- Research secondary data about the identified non-humans from various sources, aggregate actants with commonalities, and reassess their primary and secondary status in the case that the new research changes this.
- Compile research into an archetypical representation, including the non-human's species, age, lifespan, habitat, local population, needs and motivations, food and sources, challenges and stressors, and who they interact with.

3. Form a Coalition

Form a Coalition of experts to validate and refine the personas:

- Collate a list of local top-down and bottom-up initiatives related to the non-humans
- Invite these representatives to a focus group to gain primary insight and refine the secondary research
- Refine the personas to a point where the design team don't need to refer back to the Coalition, accept at times for prototype testing

4. Using personas

Use the personas to:

- View the project from the persona's perspective
- Assess the impact of the design on the non-human's needs
- Prompt workshop participants to view, critique, and ideate from the non-human's perspective
- Look for opportunities to:

  o Evaluate how non-humans might interact with the project
  o Consider long-term impacts
  o Reduce negative impacts
  o Enhance positive impacts
  o Determine any new data the non-humans that could be used

This framework was then used to retrospectively assess the following two design projects.

Project 2—An interface on the outside of an autonomous vehicle (AV)

Non-humans actants: Domestic animals, bats

Frequency of use: A retrospective analysis

Examples of non-human personas informing digital design decisions:

- *Add features*—Considering possums, ibises, and domestic cats and dogs as non-human actants at risk of being hit by the AV, the addition of sensors was suggested to enable the AV to also identify non-humans
- *Design for animal interaction*—Consider domestic dogs as non-humans who could accompany humans inside the vehicle and their interaction needs with the vehicle
- *Design for animal abilities*—Consider how bats' extra-sensory navigation might be impacted by the AV's technology
- *Consider non-human threats and future scenarios*—COVID-19 as a non-human might impact the scaling of use of the vehicles

Project 3—A desktop dashboard providing visualised data on citizens' opinions on urban developments

Non-human actants: Eucalyptus trees

Frequency of use: A retrospective analysis

Examples of non-human personas informing design decisions

- *Expand data sets to include non-humans*—Considering the eucalyptus tree as a primary non-human in urban areas due to its importance as a habitat for other species, the dashboard's algorithms could be designed to include posts and commentary about local non-human species

Other insight

- Personas are as much a method as a tool
- Identifying and defining personas can be iterative, defining new ones and redefining their status (primary and secondary) throughout the process

App interface design (Australia)

Isabella Bain

Lead Designer of the FrogID app and former Design Director at IBM Australia

Martin Tomitsch

Head of the Transdisciplinary School at University of Technology Sydney

This insight is from an analysis of "Designing for Personas That Don't Have a Voice: Reflections on Designing a Mobile Application for Collecting Biodiversity Data"—4th Australian Conference on Human-Computer Interaction, 2022

Project—FrogID App

Frog species have been slowly declining due to environmental changes and disease. In Australia, more than 20 percent are considered endangered. To raise awareness, and to enable citizens to help gather data, the Australian Museum partnered with IBM Australia to create the FrogID app, a public app anyone could download and use to record male frog calls.

Non-human actants*: The Litoria bella frog*

Creating personas

Using a persona approach, the design team collected data about the process to gather frog data to produce two personas—one for the frogs and one for the human data gatherer. They also created a scenario map of the journey to gather frog calls to capture how the frogs were impacted by human presence and to protect the frogs during the process.

Using personas

Frequency of use: Used at all stages of the process, from discovery to design

The design team used the scenario map as a starting point for the project to define the project scope and then as a reference during design to inform decisions.

They used the personas to represent their understanding of the frogs to be validated with experts such as conservations and biologists, and as a means of creating a shared understanding. Keeping the personas and scenario map on a common wall allowed anyone in the team to update the information as they learned about the frogs, democratising the process and allowing the personas to evolve during the process.

Examples of non-human personas informing design decisions:

- *Design for human presence*—Sensing the presence of humans as potential threat, frogs can stop calling. To address this, the design team implemented a dark colour palette to reduce light emitted from the app, and a "safe frogging pledge" that users had to commit to before being able to access the app's full features.

Other insight

- As non-humans can't be interviewed to confirm insights, designers must be careful to avoid bias by confirming assumptions with data and/or expert input
- The use of non-human personas can be extended beyond the design subject to also produce complimentary intervention such as awareness campaigns
- Sharing the personas and the process beyond the design team can create a shared understanding and assist in discussions regarding balancing costs and benefits

E-commerce UX (Australia)

Damien Lutz

UX Designer & Researcher

This insight is from "Experimenting with non-human personas and UX"—Medium, 2022

As a UX designer and researcher who has experimented with non-human and non-user personas, I include here insights from one of my own projects which informed the use of non-human/non-user personas for digital design.

Project—A design enhancement of an existing grocery ecommerce UX

Non-human actants: Nature

Frequency of use: A retrospective analysis

In a recent project, I employed behavioural design to evolve an existing grocery e-commerce UX so that it supported sustainable shopping choices for users. While the real problems are much larger—for example, reducing the world's consumption of disposable products—I used an overarching Nature persona to explore how UX could be used to support this bigger change at the user experience level.

Creating personas

Due to the guerrilla approach of my personal projects, I based this persona on secondary research of data.

I summarised the insight with a summary written in first person from Nature's perspective to give them a voice like any human or business actant, and so that when read by a designer it would help them empathise with Nature—like a mental preparation/meditation—and to challenge the design from Nature's needs.

Using personas

1. Empathise with the non-human/non-user's needs and problems—My first step was to read the persona to empathise with Nature as a legitimate stakeholder by focusing on their needs and problems
2. Use the non-human persona as a lens—With Nature's needs in mind, I reviewed the design to identify how it directly or indirectly impacted the

non-human needs or contributed to its problems. As the Nature persona was very generalised, I assessed how its needs/values were challenged by impacts of the industries that the digital experience supported:

- o Livestock welfare
- o Depletion of fish and sea life
- o Farmland health, soil health, etc.
- o Pesticide use
- o Agriculture disruption to natural habitats
- o Supply chain energy use and pollution
- o Excess packaging and waste

3. Relate impacts to citizen activity—I then related these issues to human citizen activity at a system level, which at its most simplistic was that citizen overconsumption was worsening all of the above impacts

4. To start connecting this systemic level issue to the digital user experience, I explored insights from earlier user testing that revealed how consumers were disconnected from caring about the system-level impacts:

- o Users felt time-poor and wanted to purchase quickly and easily
- o Users responded better when incentivised or disincentivised

5. I then brainstormed how the *business* could use its value and influence to support sustainable user behaviour rather than supporting the linear lifecycle of *take-make-waste*.

- o Slow down—*Offer discounted passes* for massages, meditation, etc.
- o Connect to nature—Suggest *weekly tips* about local nature walks to customers via weekly email, etc.
- o Connect users to where their food came from—*Collaborate* with farms to offer farm tours
- o Reduce the damage—To reduce food wastage, *offer guidance* such as setting up cooking classes on how to maximise food use and provide guides on how to donate excess food
- o Reward—*Use an existing rewards system* to encourage sustainable user behaviours
- o Heal the damage—To heal the damage of waste products ending up in landfill, *promote or facilitate* litter clean-up days (this could earn participants rewards such as points to use on more planet-friendly activities or to purchase only planet-friendly products)

6. I then brainstormed how the *UX* could support the above business initiatives, for example:

- *Filters*—Filter planet-friendly and local-made products so users can support local produce
- *Promote supporting initiatives*:
  - Link to helpful behaviour-change information such as guides to keeping food fresh for longer and tips for switching to plant-based foods
  - Promote and integrate not-for-profit and environmental organisations and events
- *Copy*—Use persona first-person voice in copy such as in pop-up modals and emails, thanking users for their planet-friendly choices, and displaying any measurable impact their choices have made
- Colour—Use calm colours and messaging (instead of time-based and urgent messaging, such as 'Buy now' or 'Low stock') to help users slow down and make time for sustainable decision making

Introducing non-human personas to clients (Europe)

Ben Serbutt

Design Lead | &us

Fiona Tout

Senior Product Designer | &us

Interviewed 2022

Introducing the use of non-human personas into commercial design practice can be tricky, so I spoke to two designers who have made a start.

&us is an innovation and transformation consultancy based in the UK. They are at the beginning of their journey into designing more life-centred, so their story about how they began using the personas gave insight into getting started with clients.

Ben Serbutt, Design Lead at *&us*, has initiated life-centred thinking with colleagues through demos and fortnightly discussions about how to incorporate life-centred thinking into their commercial design projects.

Product designer, Fiona Tout, saw one such opportunity to use a persona for nature with a recent client.

&us were helping with the UX foundations and redefining of a product for a client with a traditional waterfall mindset. During a workshop to explore the value and benefits of the product, one of the participants noted that the product contributed to the circular economy, and Fiona saw this as an opportunity to propose using a non-human persona.

After asking the client if they'd heard about life-centred design, Fiona proposed exploring the idea to use a non-human persona to represent the environment in an ideation session, which the client was very open to. Fiona framed the proposal as experimental, as it was also new for them as designers, and this gave open permission for the team to explore the concept.

Identifying non-humans/non-users

Fiona pre-determined Mother Nature as the non-human, to represent the actant of the circular economy, as mentioned by the client.

Creating personas

Using a simplified persona template on an online whiteboard, Fiona prefilled the persona with nature's behaviours and ambitions from desktop research.

The team then answered questions from the Planet Centric Design toolkit to brainstorm nature's needs and frustrations. They investigated the planet-positive and negative effects of the product, what experts they might need to bring into the project, how to measure success with nature's needs in mind.

At time of writing, &us planned to do a follow-up workshop to turn the insights into actionable items to make the product more life-centred.

Other insight

- The client was so interested in the outcomes they then aimed to use life-centred thinking in future projects.
- As a result from this positive client response, &us also aim to embed non-human personas and other life-centred strategies into their standard process for every project, especially where there might be opportunities to work with clients' sustainability and innovation departments.

Part 3
-
Learning from Interspecies Design

Introduction

During my early research into life-centred design, I noticed consideration for design impacts on animals was underrepresented when compared to consideration for environments, as animals were often considered as part of the environment.

Mobility and human-like sentience, however, give animals specific needs and abilities that are different from 'fixed' environments, making our relationship with animals unique from our relationship with environments. Considering also that animal personhood and rights are evolving on the legal front, how do designers ensure their personas capture animal-specific needs and information so their designs respect ways of being unique to animals?

"The greatness of a nation and its moral progress can be judged by the way its animals are treated."— Mahatma Gandhi

Interspecies design

To champion multi-species ways of living on the planet, interspecies design is an emerging practice that explores the design consideration of animals.

Interspecies design began with Animal Computer Interaction design and now combines with Animal Architecture and Posthumanism.

Two key streams of consideration appear to have emerged (with much overlap):

- **Respect**—Designing solutions for human problems that respect and protect animal ways of living
- **Engage**—Design solutions to be used by animals, whether via human-led or animal-initiated experiences and for specie-to-specie and cross-species interaction

Designing to respect

Two examples of design solutioning to respect the needs of animals:

- *Window material to prevent bird collisions*—The transparent and reflective nature of windows in buildings have caused millions of bird deaths, and continue to do so. Students at the Sustainable Design School in Nice utilised the unique optical attributes of a few species of birds to invent a window material with properties only the birds would notice to help them avoid collisions
- *Biodegradable and edible can ring holders*—Plastic ring holders for drink cans have created perilous dangers for wildlife and sea life getting entangled, and with fatal consequences. Saltwater Brewery, a craft beer brand based in Florida, worked with We Believers, an ad company based in NY, to produce biodegradable six-pack rings from the by-products of the beer brewing process, such as barley and wheat, meaning animals could eat them and benefit from their nutrients

The Interspecies Toolkit

Alan Hook, Senior Lecturer, Researcher, and 'maker of experiences and oddities for Human and Non-Human Animals', designs prototypes with animals to propagate interspecies empathy, with a focus on utilising an animal's love for play.

Hook also worked with Microsoft to develop the Interspecies Design Toolkit as a Speculative Design proposal complementing the Microsoft Inclusive Design Toolkit. The toolkit helps structure this emerging practice by defining various areas for consideration.

Design principles

- Recognise exclusion
- Learn from other species
- Design with one, speculate for many

The species spectrum

- Human
- Domestic
- Livestock
- Captive
- Wild

Human engager personas

Below is an elaboration of the toolkit's human personas that represent human-animal engagement:

- Farmer
- Animal Welfare
- Consumer
- Captive parent
- Pet parent
- Hunter

Types of Animal exclusion

- Physical—the relationship between physical traits and abilities (e.g. arms, legs, etc.) and interaction methods (e.g., using hands versus using beak) and the physicality of human designs (e.g., product, service, architectural, etc.)
- Cognitive—comprehension and communication
- Social—the presence of animals being recognised and respected by humans

Simulating animal abilities

Innovators have also explored the use of experience simulators to help humans empathise with experiences unique to animals.

Animal Superpowers

Animal Superpowers by Chris Woebken and Kenichi Okada was a series of wearables designed for kids to experience abilities unique to animals like magnifying vision to see like an ant.

Interface Masks

Interface Masks by Jose Chavarria swapped a human sense with animal senses like echolocation, Infrared Sensing, and Geomagnetoception for users to experience how animals perceive the world.

Designing to engage

While animals have interacted with technology since the 1960's, Animal-Computer Interaction (ACI) was first introduced in 2011 by Clara Mancini.

Animal-computer interaction design explores how human technology affects animal experiences with the aim to improve their welfare, support their activities, and foster interspecies relationships. This is to inform interspecies design as well as research ethics, such as using kind and safe wearables to collect data on animals.

Exploration into technology for animals has already produced interaction innovations such as nose plate interfaces, biteable pulleys, paw-activated buttons, and haptic vests, but this research was mostly based on human-initiated interactions.

In 2019, Ilyena Hirskyj-Douglas (a Lecturer/Assistant Professor in Animal-Computer Interaction in Scotland) and Andrés Lucero (an Associate Professor of Interaction Design in Finland) delved into animal-led interactions. They explored interconnectivity for dogs with their dog-to-dog internet project. Designing Technology for Dog-to-Dog Interaction progressed their earlier work on dog technology within the home to explore animal entertainment and well-being in scenarios such as enhancing the lives of pets left at home.

Observe and empathise

To empathise with animals, the Interspecies Design toolkit suggests observing animals to learn about their interaction needs which can prompt innovation, particularly from less considered perspectives:

- Non-verbal communication—Designers can first warm up by role-playing with friends as an animal to get familiar with non-verbal communication.
- Animal initiated interaction—If you have a pet or legal access to safe interaction with an animal, designers can practice empathising with animals, by allowing their pet to initiate and lead play, following its lead, to explore how that interaction is different from the usual experience of human-led interaction.

Observe to identify

Similarities and mismatches with human behaviours can then be used as prompts for innovation by exploring:

- Trust factors between humans and animals

- How do animals complete the same or similar tasks to humans?
- Barriers to animal accessibility to engage/interact with humans and the human world
- The animal's types of interaction and which are most common (e.g. noise, licking, touching, brushing against others, etc.)
- How do animals sense and navigate environments, and how do these abilities change with different environments?
- What elicits different types of responses?

Types of ACI systems to employ

- Screen and Tracking Systems
- Haptic and Wearable Systems
- Tangible and Physical Systems

Types of play to leverage

- Behavioural research has identified three main types of animal play:

  o Social
  o Locomotor-rotational
  o Inanimate object play

Informing animal persona design

Insights from Interspecies design can inform what to understand about animals, and what to include in their personas, in the following ways:

- Protect—Gathering information for designing products and experiences in a way that recognises and minimises potential impacts on animals, by understanding their needs to thrive and where the product/business impacts the animal
- Engage—Gathering information for designing experiences that the animal engages or interacts with by understanding how they navigate, communicate, and interact with the world, and clarifying their barriers to engagement and inclusion

Engaging the environment

On further reflection, if we can design to *engage* animals, how we might expand environment personas to include:

- How environments and non-animals like trees interact with the world and how we might interact with them rather than just take and use them?
- What processes do non-animals use to communicate (e.g., trees use fungi in their roots to communicate with other trees) that we should be aware of during design?

These considerations were taken into account for the design of the non-human/non-user **Persona Template** used in this Guide's methods.

Part 4
-
Persona methods and other uses

Introduction

Physical or digital?

While designing for physical things (physical products and services) and designing for digital experiences (websites, apps, etc.) follow a similar process, stages 1, 2, 5, and 6 vary, so a method is outlined for each practice separately for ease of reference.

How the methods were created

The methods in this book were created by synthesising insights from:

- Interviews with designers from Germany, UK, Spain, and US who had used non-human/non-user personas
- Analysis of the detailed work of academic and business projects
- My own experimentation with the creation and use of non-human/non-user personas for digital and physical products and businesses
- Workshops with students and designers

Drafts of the methods were tested and iterated via:

- A redesign of a hypothetical mattress product and business to consider the river systems impacted by production and waste
- A new experience design for Instagram to champion the reduction of the e-waste that high-usage social media platforms contribute to

See the **Sample Projects** in the virtual **Journey Backpack** at *lifecentred.design*.

While the method examples are based on retrospectively assessing existing designs, both methods can also be easily adapted to the design of a new product or business.

Three approaches to the methods

While there is an ideal complete approach to identifying, creating, and using personas, it will not always be practical for every project team to adhere to.

For example, Martin Tomitsch's excellent suggestion to create a coalition of experts to refer to would greatly increase accuracy and impact of innovations. However, not all projects will have the time and budget to achieve this level of detail and engagement with the right people.

So, the methods can be used with three different approaches:

1. Hypothetical—Useful for a fast and simplified initial inquiry and/or learning approach.

Follow the Key Steps by hypothesising and including some basic research.

If you just want to do an initial exploration and practice with the method, but don't have a product in mind, choose any subject you feel comfortable with—it could be a product in your business, an item you own, a product you want to improve. Empty the contents of your day bag or your desk drawer and look for something common, ubiquitous, and not too complex.

2. Key Steps—Useful for teams with some limitations on time, budget, and resources.

The Key Steps involve researching to inform the method with evidence-based data. As it is only secondary research, however, there's a higher risk of inaccuracy and unintended impacts. But by remaining evidence-based and using future-thinking tools such as the **Impact Ripple Canvas**, this approach has shown to still be effective in reducing impacts of design.

Also, aim to involve people from other areas of the business during the process as much as possible. Run a *How Might We?* workshop with them to generate ideas for innovating solutions. If their time is limited, try to share at least your completed Persona and artefacts with them to get their thoughts, ideas, and to understand what's important to the business.

Note: The Key Steps in these methods don't assess the energy used throughout the lifecycle as that is generally addressed by a business plan for carbon reduction and/or a transition to renewable energy.

3. Expert Steps—For a more thorough ecosystem view informed by experts.

These steps include secondary and primary research (such as interviews with experts, scientists, biologists, etc.), participatory design, and/or forming a coalition of experts to inform decisions with as much scientific data as possible. The Expert Steps also research the partners along the lifecycle and their locations.

- **Include/interview experts**—Experts may include people from industry, material and product processing and manufacturing, recycling organisations, scientists, biologists, representatives of NGOs working in the environmental sector, fact-based activists, etc.
- **Participatory research and design** (PRD)—PRD is a way of including relevant industry experts, scientists, non-users, and community knowledge bearers in the design process as legitimate design team members.
- **Forming a coalition**—Form a coalition of experts by identifying and contacting experts and initiatives from all levels of industry and

government to form a group that can advise during the process to validate your research, refine the personas, and to be available for testing prototypes.

These approaches are a guide, you can mix as you please.

Just always keep in mind the more impact your output will have, the higher the level of persona data validation you will need.

Your Journey Backpack

The tools and resources you need for both methods have been collated into a virtual backpack for your journey into the realm of non-human/non-user persona creation and use which can be accessed at *lifecentred.design*.

What's in the backpack?

Journey Maps

As previously mentioned, the creation and use of non-human/non-user persons can be a journey, and every journey needs a map!

There are two maps—one for the innovation of physical things and another for innovating digital things.

The maps list the stages of the methods and the tools you'll need so you'll always know where you are on your journey and where you're going.

Persona Library

Your Journey Backpack also includes a curated collection of persona documents, video and audio versions, and other artefacts for inspiration.

Toolkit

Your toolkit contains all the design tools you'll need for both methods:

- **Product and Service Lifecycle Maps**—Capturing research about the lifecycle activities of your product/service and their impacts on non-humans/non-users
- **Persona Research Canvas**—Capturing research about the non-humans/non-users
- **Persona Template**—Synthesising non-humans/non-user research into persona documents
- **Product Lifecycle Innovation Canvas, Caretaker Innovation Canvas, Digital Business Innovation Canvas**—Capturing existing innovations and brainstorming new ones
- **Innovation Refinement Canvas**—Collating and refining innovation ideas into statements
- **Priority Grid**—Assessing the potential impact of innovation ideas against their feasibility
- **Digital Behaviour Solutions Canvas, Digital Journey Solutions Canvas**—Exploring where and how innovations can be supported in digital channels
- **Impact Ripple Canvas**—Exploring the future potentials and unintended consequences of innovations
- **Research Guide**—Tips for accurate and efficient researching

Journey Backpack

69

Method 1 — Innovating physical things

The non-human/non-user actants in your product or service might be glaringly obvious.

For example, a book manufacturer demands paper as a resource, which causes the problem of depleting the non-human 'Trees & Forests'.

However, non-human/non-user actants can also be resources used in the production of your product's materials or in other phases of the supply chain, or the people, animals, and environments impacted throughout its lifecycle, such as farms affected by factory chemical run-off.

As an example, for mattresses made of cotton and rubber, these non-humans can at first seem like the main non-humans to consider. However, the production processes that convert these raw materials into cotton covers and latex padding use a lot of water, the chemical run-off can pollute rivers, and—at the other end of the lifecycle—the millions of mattresses discarded each year can pollute nearby water systems.

This simplified lifecycle analysis reveals that 'River Systems' are another key non-human actant to consider.

To uncover such unseen non-human/non-users, this method starts by researching the lifecycle of a physical product (or service) to create a visual map of non-humans/non-users. The also helps determine the most impacted and prompts areas for innovation.

The method also looks beyond the product lifecycle to explore how the business can use its influence and ecosystem to respect and regenerate non-humans/non-users over time.

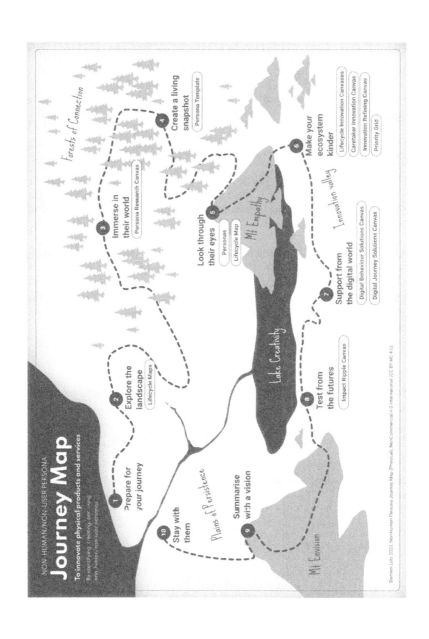

Figure 2 - Journey Map (Product/service)

Method 1 Summary

The method consists of 10 stages:

1. **Prepare for your journey**—Decide the subject, define the product materials to map, and choose how detailed your approach will be

2. **Explore the landscape**—Map the lifecycle and impacts of your product or service and the main materials to discover the impacted non-humans/non-users

3. **Immerse in their world**—Research your non-humans/non-users

4. **Create a living snapshot**—Synthesise your research into Personas and other artefacts

5. **Look through their eyes**—Apply the Personas as lenses to detail how the product lifecycle impacts non-human/non-users

6. **Make your ecosystem kinder**—Innovate to fix the lifecycle impacts and transform the business into a caretaker for the non-humans/non-users

7. **Support from the digital world**—Explore how you can support your innovations in your digital channels

8. **Test from the futures**—Explore potential future impacts of your innovations to reduce unintended consequences

9. **Summarise with a vision**—Create a visual summary to synthesise and share your regenerative vision

10. **Stay with them**—Determine metrics to measure the innovations' impact on the non-humans/non-users, embed their needs in your handover process, and evolve the personas over time

*Note: A **Time** is shown at each stage—this approximates how long it might take to complete just the Key Steps.*

1. Prepare for your journey

You peer out over the vast landscape awaiting your exploration, humbled by nature's complex balance and excited by what you'll see and learn.

Summary

To prepare, you'll identify the main materials of your subject to map.

Time: 10-20 mins

Persona Tools: None

Identify the product materials

To map the lifecycle of a physical product, you need to identify a few of its main materials so you can map what happens to them from when they are taken out of nature to when they are returned.

Select materials that make up the bulk of your product and packaging. As a start, aim for 1-3 product materials plus 1 packaging material.

For example, a mattress business would determine the materials of its main parts, such as cotton for the covering, rubber for the latex padding, steel for the coils, and plastic or cardboard for the packaging.

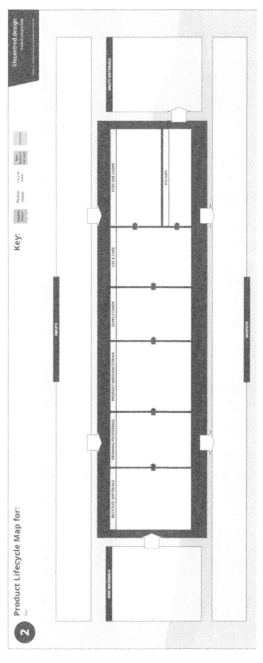

Figure 3 - Product Lifecycle Map

76

2. Explore the landscape

Hitching your backpack over your shoulders, you explore the landscape to map its complexities and learn about its lifeforms and their interconnectedness.

Summary

Using the **Product Lifecyle Map**, you'll create a visual map of your product's lifecycle by researching what happens to the main materials and what resources are used, from which you can then identify the impacted non-humans/non-users.

Time: 1-2 hrs

Method Tools: Product Lifecycle Map

Design Modes: Research and Visual Mapping

Key Steps:

1. Empathise
2. Map the lifecycle of the product and its materials, and the inputs, outputs and impacts
3. Identify the primary non-humans/non-users

Expert Steps:

- Map *all* the materials of your product
- Map the broader ecosystem:

  o Note all the organisations involved in the lifecycle (e.g., mining companies and farmers that produce the raw materials, factories that transform the materials into parts and products, and supply chain organisations, etc.) and learn about their environments and the human communities and animals that live there

  o Visit the physical environments of each lifecycle phase and ecosystem to observe and interview

  o Consider also what resources your business uses on a day-to-day basis, and where those materials come from

- Interview experts

1. Empathise

Take five minutes to connect with the present and Nature. Use a technique below to empathise with Nature and feel gratitude for how it supports your life, your energy flow, and all life on Earth.

- Try a slow breathing approach, recognising how the flow of air connects you to the world as it moves in and out of you and everything else
- Talk a walk or open a window and notice the sounds, the smells, the feel of the air, the textures of plants, the movement of clouds, any animals and insects
- Find a quiet spot under a tree, by a lake, or where you can lay back and watch the clouds move, the life in the tree branches, or around the lake
- Try a short meditation from an online source or use an imagination exercise, for example:

Imagine your body as Nature, the Earth, your blood are the rivers, your muscles the soil, your skin the land, and your breathing the wind.

Imagine humanity as a small lifeform present in your body, a part of your system, but expanding rapidly and overdrawing from your blood and your nutrients, blocking blood and airflow, and congesting your veins and lungs.

Breath slow and deep and imagine harmonising with humanity, and humanity harmonising with you in return, forming a symbiotic relationship where energy flows freely so you both thrive.

2. Map the lifecycle

Now that you're more open to the needs of life beyond humanity's needs, map the lifecycle of your materials and product on the **Product Lifecycle Map**.

About the Product Lifecycle Map

The **Product Lifecycle Map** represents the phases of a product lifecycle and the lifecycle's inputs and outputs.

In the centre of the map is the black *Contained Lifecycle* area—all the activities involved in the lifecycle happen in this area, from sourcing recycled materials and manufacturing to consumer use, discard, and post-use loops of resell, refurbish, and recycle.

Surrounding the *Contained Lifecycle* are the inputs and outputs—everything from nature that is taken in by the lifecycle, and everything that goes back out into nature.

The lifecycle phases consist of:

- **Raw materials, Recycled materials, and the Processing of materials**—How the product materials are extracted from nature and how these raw materials are processed into new materials (e.g., iron ore is processed into steel), and if any recycled materials are used
- **Product Manufacturing**—How the processed materials are manufactured into products
- **Supply Chain**—How products are distributed around the world, from factory to sales points (retail, wholesale, etc.), and how they are delivered to the customer
- **Use and care**—How a customer uses the product, how they care for it, any parts or add-ons they may purchase and use during their ownership, and how it is repaired
- **Post-use loops**—How products or materials get more than one life after the user is finished with them, if it is repurposed, resold, donated, refurbished for resale, or recycled
- **Discard and Waste**—How products or materials become waste, how they might be thrown away and/or end up in landfill or nature

Nature's inputs:

- **Raw materials**—The natural materials used to make the parts for your product, such as cotton grown for mattress covers
- **Lifecycle resources**—The 'resources' from nature that are used to enable the lifecycle activities, such as river water for irrigating cotton fields

Lifecycle outputs:

- **Lifecyle output**—Output from the lifecycle activities, such as material waste, biodegradable waste, pollution, etc. Also consider invisible outputs like excessive heat, noise, magnetic fields, etc.
- **Product waste**—What becomes of the product, parts, and materials if they are not kept in the Contained Lifecycle. (e.g., end up in landfill)

Brainstorm

Before you research, brainstorm what you think happens across the lifecycle, capturing notes on the **Product Lifecycle Map.** This is a good soft start to product lifecycle mapping and generates ideas of where to start researching.

Use the map's Key in the top right of the map to colour code your stickies.

Start by using sticky notes to note the main materials that you identified in *Stage 1—Prepare for your journey* on the **Product Lifecycle Map.** Place them in the *Raw Materials* or *Recycled Materials* areas. Include any other information you may know about them, and:

- Hypothesise what happens to the materials and the product through the lifecycle, including inputs and outputs
- Hypothesise what people and environments are impacted and how:
  - **Negative**—How are humans, animals, and environments hurt, depleted, disrespected, etc.?
  - **Positive**—How do humans, animals, and nature benefit from the lifecycle at any phase? (e.g., the business may pay for factory workers' health care, perhaps waste is used as compost to regenerate soil, etc.)

Research

Once you've exhausted your brainstorming, start researching to validate your ideas and to fill in the knowledge gaps. (Don't forget to read the **Research Guide** in the toolkit for best research practices.)

Continue to add sticky notes to your **Product Lifecycle Map**, research what happens from when the materials are first obtained (extracted from the Earth and/or drawn from recycled materials) to what happens to them and the product after the product is finished with (recycled, ends up in landfill, etc.).

Capture notes and images to make it a visually rich map. Infographics are also useful to summarise detail, such as production processes, etc.

This mapping can get messy—let that happen, have fun it, and tidy up at the end if it's easier.

How detailed you get is up to you, but the deeper you research, the more accurate your insight and the more meaningful your innovations will be. Research too shallow, and your innovations may even have unintended consequences (but you'll try to mitigate that at *Stage 8—Test from the futures*).

As you research, you may come across innovation ideas—capture these, but you'll explore these in more detail later after you've chosen which non-humans/non-users to innovate for.

What to look for in your research:

- Material extraction/sourcing and processing

  o The origin of your key materials—what part of nature do they come from?
  o A summary of how they are processed into usable materials (e.g., sap from a rubber tree is processed into latex)
  o Note the benefits of materials and processes, such as materials that are sustainable, treatments making materials mould and fire resistant, etc.
  o Note inputs (e.g., water for irrigation) and outputs

- Parts and product manufacturing

  o A summary of the parts/product manufacturing and packaging process.
  o Note inputs (e.g., water for processing) and outputs

- Distribution and sales

  o How is your product distributed to sales channels?
  o Note inputs and outputs (While the insight for this stage might be mainly about the energy use and pollution of the supply chain, which is not a focus of the Key Steps of this method, your business may have choice over which providers and methods it uses to change providers)

- Consumer use and care

  o How do your customers receive/obtain their product?
  o Note any significant products or activities required by consumers to use and care for the product
  o Note inputs (e.g., wax for polishing furniture) and outputs (packaging)

- Post-use loops

  o Note how consumers can keep the product in circular loops— donating, reselling, refurbishing, and recycling
  o Note if and how the product is collected for these loops
  o Note human behaviours and product/business/system features here that enable and encourage the post-use loops
  o Note inputs (e.g., water for recycling) and outputs

- Discard
  - How do consumers otherwise discard the product, such as binning, taking it to city waste centres, and what ends up in landfill?
  - Note human behaviours and product/business/system features that encourage and enable this behaviour, such as how the size of a product makes it difficult to dispose of responsibly, etc.

- Waste materials
  - Note if any parts of your product end up as landfill or environmental waste and how much
  - Note inputs required here (e.g., land for landfill) and outputs (e.g. chemical leaching into soil and rivers)

Mapping a service

If your business facilitates a *service* in the physical world, you can use personas to innovate the lifecycle of the service activities and the materials uses. The method is the same as for mapping a physical product with a few tweaks and using the **Service Lifecycle Map** instead.

Identify the main materials

For a service, select materials that make up the bulk of the products used to deliver the service. As a start, aim for 1-3 product materials.

For example, a cleaning service might determine the main materials for its cleaning products (e.g., water for cleaning liquids) or equipment (e.g., oil for plastic). And a bicycle-sharing business might determine the main materials to be aluminum for bike frames and rubber for tires.

About the Service Lifecycle Map

The **Service Lifecycle Map** is a simplified view of the materials used, service activities that occur, and impacts of both in the delivery of the service.

Phases of a service lifecycle consist of:

- **Raw materials**—The raw materials used to make the products and equipment used in the service
- **Processing/manufacturing**—How the materials are processed into new materials to create the products and equipment used in the service (e.g., oil is processed into plastic)
- **Product/Equipment**—Any products and equipment used in the service
- **Service Sequence**—The steps of the service, from beginning to completion
- **Post-use loops**—Any ways the service products or equipment get more than one life when the service is finished with them
- **Discard and Waste**—How the service products or equipment become unused waste, if they end up in landfill or dumped in nature

Brainstorm

Hypothesise what happens to the materials and the products and equipment through the lifecycle. Note what you know about any activities throughout the delivery of the service, including inputs and outputs, what people and environments they might impact, and how.

Research

Continuing to add sticky notes to your **Service Lifecycle Map**, research what happens from when the product/equipment materials are first obtained (extracted from the Earth and/or drawn from recycled materials) to what happens to them and the product after the product is finished with (recycled, ends up in landfill, etc.). Research any gaps about the service sequence you may not know, such as impacts of any outputs like chemical waste, etc.

- Material extraction
  - The origin of your key materials—what part of nature do they come from?
- Processing/ manufacturing

- o A summary of how they are processed into usable materials (e.g., oil extracted to be made into plastic)
- o A summary of the parts/product manufacturing process
- o Note inputs (e.g., water for processing) and outputs (e.g., waste, pollution)

- Service sequence

  - o Note the steps of the service, from beginning to completion
  - o Note inputs (e.g., water for cleaning) and outputs

- Post-use loops

  - o Note the ways the service products and equipment can be kept in circular loops after the service is finished with them. Are they repurposed, resold, donated, refurbished for resale, or recycled? Note if and how the product is collected for these loops.
  - o Note human behaviours and product/business/system features here that enable and encourage the post-use loops
  - o Note inputs (e.g., water for recycling) and outputs

- Discard

  - o How does the service otherwise discard the products and equipment, such as binning, taking to city waste centers, etc.
  - o Note human behaviours and product/business/system features that encourage and enable this behaviour, such as how chemical waste might be difficult to dispose of responsibly, etc.

- Waste materials

  - o Note if any parts of your product end up as landfill or environmental waste
  - o Note inputs required here (e.g., land for landfill) and outputs (e.g., chemical leaching into soil and rivers)

Identify the non-users and non-humans

Once you've mapped the materials and product/service lifecycle, apply a human, animal, and environment lens to capture how the activities, inputs, and outputs impact them.

As mentioned earlier, you'll find them in these main areas:

- Used as materials *for the product parts*
- The environments, animals and people *used at each lifecycle phase* (e.g., water used during material processing, factory workers, land for landfill, etc.)
- The environments, animals and people *impacted by the lifecycle phases*

Apply a human non-user lens to identify:

- Any directly impacted people and how they are impacted (e.g., unfair pay for factory workers or exposure to chemicals, etc.)
- Any indirectly peoples (local businesses unable to compete, the indigenous community's way of life disturbed, etc.)

Apply a non-human environment lens to identify any used or impacted:

- o Vegetation (trees, forests, swamps, etc.)
- o Water systems (oceans, lakes, rivers, freshwater)
- o Climate and weather systems
- o Air, soil, landforms (mountains, hills, etc.), sunlight, noise

Apply a non-human animal lens to identify:

- Any animals in the environments and how they might be impacted (e.g., their food or habitat spoiled by pollution, movement restricted by fences, etc.)
- Consider large animals (amphibians, reptiles, birds, and mammals) to insects and microbes; on land, sea, air, or underground; domestic, livestock, captive, or wild; whether 'proven' sentient or not

Also consider:

- Non-living non-humans—Consider creating personas for the 'non-living' issues your product creates or contributes to, such as e-waste or landfill
- Disturbances/threats—Consider any of the above that have the potential to cause great disturbance to the product and business, such as viruses like COVID19, which you can then use these as part of a general risk assessment

3. Identify the *primary* non-humans/non-users

Identify the primary non-humans and non-users to work with.

Some primary non-humans/non-users may be very clear, but also think in terms of what's specific to your business system, and which are:

- Greatest in number
- Most negatively impacted (not just the most often)
- Most local to your system
- Most important to your system

You can also take a planetary view to help determine which is most important:

- Which have the most importance to life on Earth?
- Which are most at risk, weakened, vulnerable, and/or marginalised?
- Are any directly connected to urgent global issues (e.g., The Planetary Boundaries)?

Ensure you trace the environmental non-human to their source. For example, if a manufacturing process uses high amounts of water, this usually comes from dams, but the source might be 'The Local River Systems'.

How many personas you create depends on your purpose. You might choose one if you are just practicing, or you could choose one environment, one animal, and one human. If you're following the **Key Steps**, you might focus on the ones that are most impacted. For the **Expert Steps**, you might create personas for them all.

Product Lifecycle

3. Immerse in their world

Having spotted various lifeforms in the wild and identified those in need, you immerse yourself in their world to understand what challenges them and what makes them thrive.

Summary

You'll collect fact-based insights about your primary non-humans/non-users through research to document their place in the world, their importance, their needs and threats, and their relationship with humanity.

Time: 1-2 hrs per persona

Method Tools: Persona Research Canvas

Design Modes: Research

Key Steps:

1. Research facts
2. Pause and reflect

Expert Steps:

- Interview experts
- Form a coalition
- If given consent, study any human non-user in their environment
- If legally and safely possible, study any animal in their environment:

  o What do their behaviours tell you is important to them?
  o How does the environment treat them back?
  o If your non-human is a domestic animal, and you have legal and safe access to them, allow them to initiate and lead play and follow their lead to explore how that interaction is different from the usual experience of human-led interaction

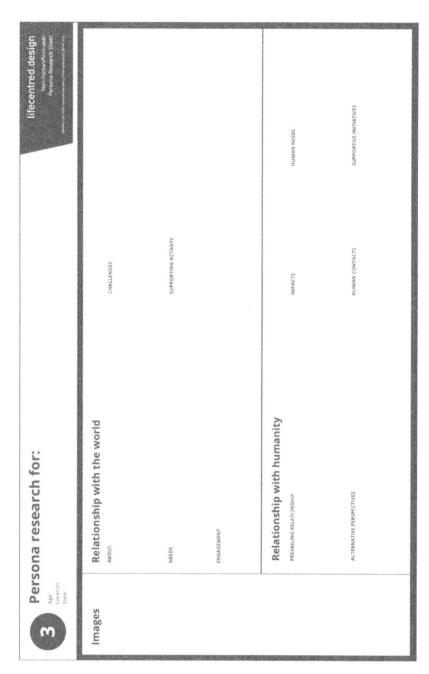

Figure 4 - Persona Research Canvas

1. Research facts

Follow the **Research Guide** for best practices, research to collect fact-based information about your non-humans/non-users on the **Persona Research Canvas**.

Below are suggestions about what information to research, based on insights from the practitioners and experiments shared earlier in this book. Feel free to include anything else that could inform design decisions specific to your project.

Collect lots of interesting bits of information, as you'll make sense of it all later. Follow tangents and immerse yourself in learning about the non-human/non-user—this researching process is as important as creating the persona.

As with researching for the **Lifecycle Map**, how deep your research goes is up to you, but you need at least enough detail to understand the non-human/nonuser's needs.

Be prepared for unexpected and/or uncomfortable emotions arising as you delve into the lives of people, plants, animals, and environments—how humanity might be treating them in terrible ways, and how your own behaviours may play a contributing role. Use this discomfort as a measure that you are going deep enough in your research to ensure you are not just identifying key needs but also getting the key benefit from creating personas—empathy. Let these emotions come up, knowing that you will harness them and their energy in positive ways in *Stage 6 – Make your ecosystem kinder*.

In fact, as you do this research, you'll most likely discover more kind and healing innovations, so note them down to come back to later.

Note: Identifying and defining personas can be iterative throughout the process. Be open to adding and pivoting to any new non-human/non-users that arise at any stage.

Start researching

Identification data

Give the persona a name, and for non-users (being humans), also give them a descriptor, such as 'Factory worker'.

Collect:

- Images—Web search or try a resource like *unsplash.com* to find a key image that:
  - o Is instantly recognisable
  - o Captures the non-human's importance 'in action'
  - o Conveys some emotion
- Age and lifespan
- Habitat locations specific to your persona, but also add where else they can be found (e.g., the River Systems in the example Persona was based in Australia, but they are found worldwide)

Relationship with the world

- **About, Needs, and Engagement**
  - o **About**
    - For non-users, gather facts and scenarios to feed into a general definition and summary of what they do, their role in the world and in the business ecosystem, and some history, quality of life, attitudes, interests, hopes, statistics, etc. Consider also if their way of existing is different to yours. For example, do they work according to the Gregorian calendar or lunar cycles (or both); do they follow any cultural cycles?
    - For non-humans, what does the non-human/non-user do for the world and why is this important? Are they part of a greater system/cycle? What other lifeforms or cycles rely on the non-human/non-user for their own healthy existence? Include key statistics. Consider what cycles they might synchronise with—for example, if they're an animal, are they diurnal or nocturnal, etc.?
  - o **Needs**—What do they need to survive and thrive (e.g., food, habitat, room for roaming or migration, etc.) If you can determine with factual evidence, include their needs for beyond basic needs to survive, such as what is known to give them joy
  - o **Engagement**—How do they interact with the world?

- Communication—How do they communicate? (e.g., plant roots use fungi to communicate with each other, and bees use dance and vibration to communicate, human workers might use Whatsapp)
- Interaction—For animals, what are their forms of interaction with world? (e.g., dogs bite to pull, monkeys climb with arms and legs, etc.). For humans, do they have any unique forms of interaction? (e.g., A blind or visually impaired person uses sound and tactile interaction methods). Plants *filter* gases (carbon and oxygen) and nutrients, rivers *move* and *pulse*.
- Navigation—For animals, how do they sense and navigate environments (e.g., bats use sonar), and how do these abilities change with different environments? For humans, do they have any unique forms of navigation? (e.g., A blind or visually impaired person might use a cane, service animal, and GPS)

  o Additional Engagement research for animal non-humans—If you are designing something for an animal to interact with, these are research questions to learn more about their behaviours and interactions:

  - How do animals complete the same or similar tasks to humans?
  - What are the animal's types of interaction, and which are most common (e.g., noise, licking, touching, brushing against others, electromagnetic, etc.)
  - What elicits different types of responses?
  - How do they communicate with each other and with lifeforms outside their specie?
  - What are their mental skills (learning, recall, solving problems, etc.)?
  - What are their routines and rituals?
  - What's a day in their life?

- **Challenges and Supporting Actants**

  o **Challenges**—What threatens their ability to obtain food and shelter, to procreate, to be valued, or to do what they need to do that makes them important in the world?

  o **Supporting Actants**—Who are the key actants that the non-human/non-user relies on for a healthy existence? Who or what enables the non-human/non-user's food, habitat, room for roaming/migration, procreation, etc? (e.g., birds need worms for food, flowers need bees to pollinate them). What are the supporters' key needs to thrive? (If any of these are significant in any way, such as essential for the survival of the primary non-human/non-user or in critical danger, you might want to make a persona for them also).

Relationship with humanity

- **Prevailing relationship and impacts**
  - What is the dominant human relationship with the non-human/non-user that has the most power over it? What is the nature of this relationship?
    - For environments and animals—Do humans engage/use/harm/nurture/exclude the non-human/non-user? (e.g., humans use rivers for recreation, food, hydration, travel, agriculture, irrigation, etc.; animals can be socially and physically excluded by human spaces); How important does humanity view and treat them? (e.g., for rivers, humans use them for drinking, food, and irrigation using regulation of the water flow, taking water, and dumping waste back into the rivers)
    - For human non-users—What is their status in society's eyes, how are they treated, included, or excluded, etc?; What are their privileges or lack of?
  - Impacts—What are the impacts of the prevailing relationship on the non-humans/non-users?

- **Alternate perspectives, Human contacts, and Supportive initiatives**
  - **Alternate perspectives**—What are less common human relationships with the non-human/non-user? Often dominance over environments and animals belongs to Euro-Western, capitalistic, development-focused peoples. If this is the case for your non-humans/non-users, what are alternate perspectives and relationships that are better for the health of their world and can be explored to improve the damaging relationships:
    - For environments and animals—How are they respected and nurtured, and who does this well? (e.g., First Nations Australians have a spiritual connection with river systems and lived with them in sustainable ways for thousands of years)
    - For human non-users—Do they have unappreciated and/or untapped value? (e.g., not just a factory worker but a world citizen deserving of foundational rights and respect). How do different organisations treat or support them?
  - **Human contacts**—Consider who most engages with your non-human/non-user:

- Examples of key human contacts for non-humans—Farmer, Animal Welfare Officer, Consumer, Captive parent, Pet parent, Hunter
- Examples of key human contacts for non-users—Boss, Delivery drivers, Support groups, Parole officer, Doctor, Neighbour

o **Supportive Initiatives**

- What are the organisations and initiatives that support the non-humans/non-users? Are there local, national, and global initiatives?
- The United Nations Sustainable Development Goals (SDGs) are 17 interconnected global goals created by the United Nations that form 'a shared blueprint for peace and prosperity for people and the planet (see *https://sdgs.un.org/goals*). What SDGs are the non-human/non-user related to?

Persona Research

2. Pause and reflect

- When you feel you're done, take a short break, and then come back to your work
- Ask yourself if there is anything missing or needs clarifying
- Gather any further research you feel is required

When you feel your research is complete, take another well-earned break, or jump into bringing your non-humans/non-users to life by compiling your research into persona documents and other artefacts.

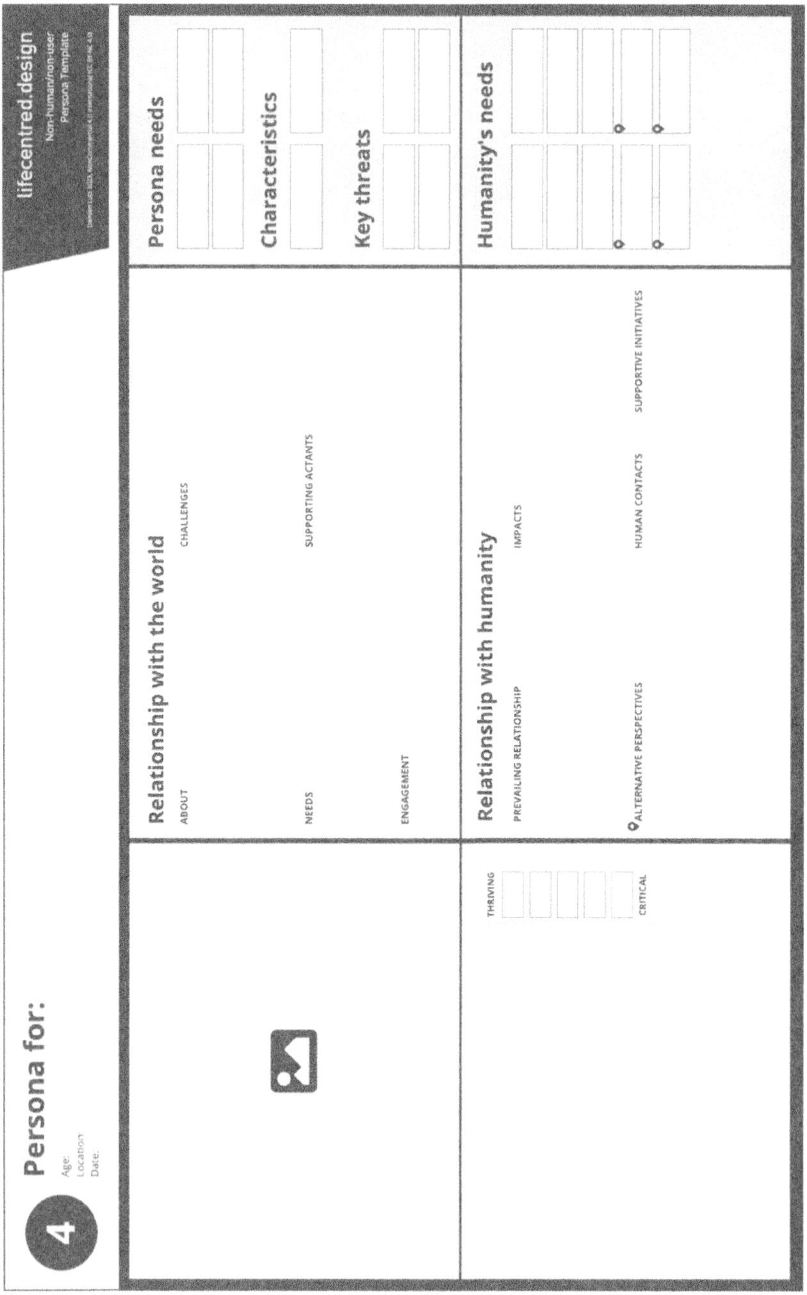

Figure 5 - Persona Template

4. Create a living snapshot

After your deep exploration of the lifeforms most in need, you take a seat on a log atop a valley edge, gaze over the landscape, and create a mental snapshot so you don't forget what you've learned about them and their needs.

Summary

Informed by your research, you'll now create the persona—a 'living snapshot' of your non-human/non-user—by synthesising your research into succinct personas that are effective for communicating the non-human/non-user's needs and perspectives during decision-making.

Time: 30-60 mins per persona

Method Tools: Persona Template

Design Modes: Synthesising and Persona Creation

Key Steps:

1. Choose how to best represent the non-human/non-user
2. Synthesise your research onto the **Persona Template**
3. Explore the need for other persona artefacts

Expert Steps:

- Co-create with the business
- Interview experts
- Share with a coalition for feedback

1. Choose the best representation

If you haven't already, decide how the non-human/non-user would best be represented:

- Individual—For a specific individual non-human/non-user
- Group—A herd/flock/etc., family, community, minority group, etc.
- Specie

2. Synthesise your research onto the Persona Template

Create 'a source of truth' persona for each non-human/non-user, one that is easily edited, readable, and sharable for feedback and collaboration.

This source of truth can then be used to create different persona artefacts in different mediums based on a project's needs (more about that later).

About the Persona Template

The template consists of five sections:

1. Identity Header
2. Empathy summary (left-hand column)
3. Relationship with the world row
4. Relationship with humanity row
5. The Needs and Threats column

1. Identity Header

Name your persona, capture its locations and age, and add the date you're creating the persona.

2. Empathy Summary

The empathy section consists of a key image, a written summary, and a health rating, with the purpose being to generate empathy for the non-human/non-user without designers and workshop participants reading all the detail.

Image

Choose an image that:
- Is instantly recognisable
- Captures the non-human's importance 'in action'
- Conveys some emotion

Written Summary

The written summary can be read at design and decision-making times to aid in remembering and *feeling* the non-human/non-user's needs.

It can be written in first person, as if the non-human/non-user is speaking, to help readers empathise—avoid over-humanising by using language that reflects their values and world. Or it can be written from an observer's perspective to ensure readers understand the persona is an outside perspective.

Health Rating

Estimate the non-human/non-user's current health rating on a rating from critical to thriving. You can use colour for emphasis and arrows to show if they are improving or worsening.

- For animals and environments, consider the species' predicament in the world, if they are declining or thriving
- For human non-users consider the quality of their life, opportunities, and if these are improving or worsening

3. Relationship with the world

Importance and Challenges

Summarise how the non-human/non-user are important to the world, and what threatens their safety and longevity.

Needs and Supporting actants

Summarise their needs to survive and thrive, and what actants support their existence and how.

Engagement

Note how they engage with the world.

Non-human/non-user needs

In the right column, summarise your non-human/non-user insight into their key needs for surviving, healing, and thriving. Include key needs for their supporters.

Key threats

Summarise the challenges into the most serious threats to the non-human/non-user.

Tips

To create a Persona that is efficient for guiding decisions:

- Simplify as much as you can without compromising the overall value of the information for decision-making
- Make the persona visual and scannable so it is easy to digest at decision-making
- Use infographics to convey complex or extraneous information more simply—UN Biodiversity on Linkedin can be a good source (*https://www.linkedin.com/company/unbiodiversity*)
- Remain fact and evidence-based and wary of stereotyping—stay vigilant against accidental embedding of stereotypes and your own bias into non-human needs and experiences
- AI can help with shaping copy, solutions, first voice, personality, and images, but check the results to be careful of incorrect facts, bias, stereotyping, etc.

4. Relationship with humanity

Prevailing relationship and Impacts

Summarise who has the most power over the non-human/non-user and what their relationship is with them—do they support them, use them, what are their attitudes toward their value, and how are they impacted?

Alternative Perspectives

Summarise alternate perspectives and relationships with your non-human/non-user, such as the Supportive Initiatives and those with less control over the dominant relationships with the humans/non-users.

Human contacts

Reviewing your research, determine the main human contact(s) for your non-human/non-user. This is to identify who might be inspiration and/or allies in assisting with innovation. If you have several to choose from, prioritise who is most closely related to your non-human's relationship with your product lifecycle.

Supportive initiatives

Reviewing your research, determine who are the main group(s) that support your non-human/non-user. Include the related United Nations Sustainable Development Goals (SDG). Again, this is to identify who might be inspiration and/or allies in assisting with innovation.

Consider what's being done at all levels:

- Macro—Initiatives working at a global level
- Meso—Initiatives working at the local level, such as organisational collaborations, local communities, etc.
- Micro—Initiatives by individuals

Humanity's needs

In the right column, summarise humanity's needs of the non-human.

For human non-user personas, summarise what humanity needs *to do* to make life better for the non-users.

Reflecting on the needs of the non-human/non-user, their supporters' needs, and humanity's needs, identify and highlight any that are common—these can be priority needs to focus on when designing.

Rivers Persona

3. Explore other artefacts

Different projects might require different persona artefacts, such as any research output that is specific for the project.

Also, multi-media versions such as video and audio can be powerful in emotionally engaging and influencing business, partners, and the public.

Determine if other artefacts might be useful for your project

Examples:

- Multi-media artefacts to engage and influence business, partners, and the public:
    - A video—this can be simple, such as one continuous shot or image with narration, or a story with sound effects
    - An audio of someone speaking in the first person of the non-human/non-user
    - A written short story

- Journey maps
    - A day/night in the life of your non-human/non-user
    - How and when humans interact with the non-human/non-user (e.g., farmer milking a cow, birdwatcher spying birds, scientists studying frogs in a stream, etc.)
    - The non-human/non-user's journey through history

- Design principles to guide micro-level design (UX, UI, etc.) and to share with other business areas such as marketing

See the **Persona Library** for examples of the above.

An Audio Persona

5. Look through their eyes

You close your eyes for a moment, and imagine being one of the lifeforms you've discovered, their needs now your needs. You open your eyes again and see the landscape in an entirely new way as if looking through their eyes, heart, and mind.

Summary

Using the persona as a lens, you'll reassess your **Lifecycle Map** through the non-human/non-user's eyes and with their needs in mind, and then transform all the problems you've found into *How Might We?* statements to prepare for innovating.

Time: 1 hr

Method Tools: Your completed Personas and Lifecycle Map

Design Modes: Brainstorming and Research

Steps:

1. Empathise
2. Reassess the lifecycle using the personas as lenses
3. Summarise with *How Might We?* statements

Expert Steps:

- Interview experts
- Share with a coalition for feedback
- Use participatory analysis

1. Empathise with the non-human/non-user

Before using the persona to assess the system for how it impacts them, use the *Empathise Summary* to connect and empathise with your non-human/non-user.

Read the *Empathy Summary* as a mediative approach by imagining being the persona, and their needs are your needs.

This immersive approach is meant to help de-centre yourself and critique the design with less bias and more from the non-human/non-user's perspective.

2. Reassess lifecycle

Using the deeper insight you now have about your non-humans/non-users, use the persona to reassess the **Lifecycle Map** for impacts:

- Confirm the impacts (and causes) to your non-human/non-user that your lifecycle mapping already identified, and add any more detail
- Referring to the Persona, brainstorm how else the lifecycle might:
  - Impact the *Non-human/non-user needs*
  - Impact the *Human needs and/or common needs*
  - Worsen the *Key Threats, Challenges* and/or *Human Impacts*
  - Challenge or hinder the *Supportive initiatives*

- Referring to the Persona, identify root causes of the problems, which may be somewhere else on the lifecycle

---

Example of root causes

Many mattresses are dumped on the street or in bin rooms from which they end up in landfill, causing pollution to soil and river systems, but the causes can originate from different lifecycle phases, for example:

- Some mattresses are designed with materials or in a way that can't be recycled (A problem at the materials/design phase)
- Dumping mattresses is easy (A problem at the Discard phase)
- Mattresses are big and bulky and hard to deliver to a recycling center (A problem at the Discard phase, but also at the Use & Care phases due to a lack of user awareness about recycling options and behaviour barriers)

---

3. Summarise with *How Might We?* statements

Time to synthesise the insights from your **Lifecyle Map** into innovation prompts.

Write a *How Might We?* statement (HMW) for all the ways your non-human/non-user is impacted.

A HMW statement rewrites a problem as question for innovation.

When writing an HMW, don't suggest a specific type of solution, keep it solution agnostic so that brainstorming is not limited to 1 type of solution.

Examples of *How Might We?* statements:

1. If the **problem** is that customers aren't aware of how they can resell, refurbish, and recycle their old mattresses, the ***How Might We?*** could be "How might we increase customer awareness about the resell, refurbish, and recycle options for mattresses?"

2. If the **problem** is that customers dump their mattresses rather than take them to a recycling facility because mattresses are hard to transport; ***How Might We?***—How might we simplify mattress transportation for customers to encourage them to choose recycling facilities over dumping?

Check that your HMW statements address all the non-humans/non-user *Needs* and *Key Threats* on the **Persona**.

By the end of this step, you should have plenty of HMW prompts to start innovating solutions to make your product and business kinder to your non-human/non-users.

Lifecycle HMW

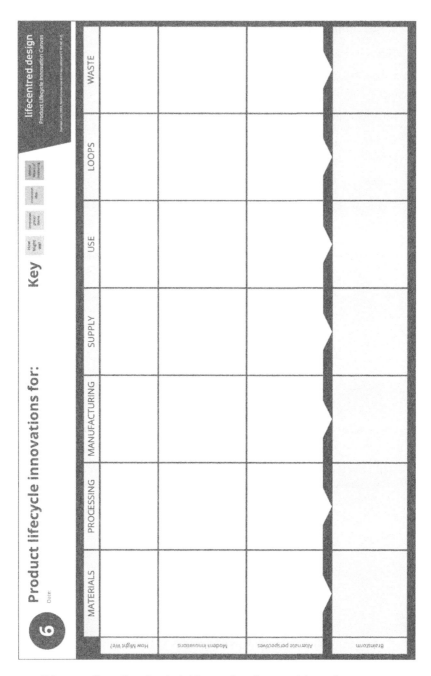

Figure 6 – Product Lifecycle Innovation Canvas

6. Make your ecosystem kinder

Infused with a deeper empathy, you seek ways to harmonise with nature, so that you become more life-centred and symbiotic with the world, take only what is needed, and regenerate the landscape and its lifeforms.

Summary

Using the *How Might We?* statements as prompts, you'll first research related solutions from your industry and beyond to then brainstorm how you not only redesign your lifecycle but also become an ongoing caretaker to advocate for the non-human/non-user's thriving existence.

Time: 1-2 hrs

Method Tools: Completed Personas, Product Lifecycle Innovation Canvas, Caretaker Innovation Canvas, Innovation Refining Canvas

Design Modes: Research, Brainstorming, Insight synthesising

Steps:

1. Research innovations
2. Brainstorm innovations
3. Refine ideas
4. Prioritise

Expert Steps:

- Interview experts
- Share with a coalition for feedback
- Use participatory design

1. Research innovations

Place your *How Might We?* statements on the **Lifecycle Innovation Canvas** in the top row under the relevant Lifecycle phases.

Following the **Research Guide** for best research practices, research innovation ideas. Innovations can happen at three levels:

- **Lifecycle innovations (Meso)**—Solutions at any stage of the lifecycle that solve the *How Might We?* statements, while still providing the desired solution. For example, mattress materials can be synthetic and/or treated with chemicals to make them mould and fire resistance—what organic materials provide the same resistance?
- **Regenerative innovations (Macro)**—Solutions that give back to the impacted actants, such as donating to conservation organisations, etc., to ensure they thrive into the future
- **User innovations (Micro)**—Nudges to sustainable human behaviours in both customers and citizens

Product Lifecycle Innovation Canvas

Research and capture on your **Product Lifecycle Innovation Canvas** the following:

- **Modern innovations**
  - **Your industry**—How have other businesses already solved your lifecycle problems through removing, reducing, and/or restoring the impacts?
  - **Other industries**—Look at what organisations from any industry are doing to improve lifecycle, be regenerative, and/or nudge human behaviour
  - **Certified standards**—Look at certified standards from credible and independent third-party eco-labelling schemes for what to achieve
  - **Technology**—What new and emerging technologies in your industry could you leverage? What about technologies from beyond your industry? Try future signal tools such as *https://techdetector.de/radar*
  - **Artificial Intelligence**—Drawing from collective human knowledge, what does AI say? Try different AI tools and use the ideas to prompt investigation. Always check the validity of AI responses as their data bases can be limited and biased

- **Alternate perspectives**

  - ○ **First Nations Wisdom**—Have older cultures such as First Nations Peoples resolved a similar problem in some way?
  - ○ **Natural Intelligence**—Using biomimicry and a resource like *asknature.org*, explore how plants, environments, and animals have solved 'design' problems in sustainable and waste-free ways
  - ○ **Non-conventional Innovation**—Explore 'frugal engineering' and resolving problems with few resources or only what is at hand, such as DIY, hacking, and the Southeast Asian practice of *Jugaad*

Caretaker Innovation Canvas

Now using the **Caretaker Innovation Canvas**, go wider by researching how the *Supportive initiatives* and *Alternate perspectives* (from your Persona) support and nurture the non-human/non-user in such ways as:

- **Heal past and steer futures**—What is being done to heal the damage done to the non-human/non-user, and what is being done to invest in both short term and long-term support?
- **Collaborate and share**—Are any organisations collaborating and sharing information or resources to support the non-human/non-user?
- **Inform and enable**—How are users and/or citizens informed about the impacts to the non-human/non-user, and are they encouraged in any way to act differently or support?

When researching innovations, think in terms of:

- **Modern innovations**

  - ○ **Industry innovation**—How are other businesses donating, investing, supporting, etc. their non-humans/non-users? Look at their corporate websites and sustainable sections and reports.
  - ○ **Supportive initiatives**—Research how the *Supportive initiatives* nurture and conserve your non-humans/non-users to capture their conservation strategies and ways for mitigating the *Threats* and *Human Impacts* (from the Persona)
  - ○ **Technology**—Are any specific or emerging technologies beneficial to supporting the activities above or the non-human/non-user directly?

- **Alternate Perspectives**

  - ○ Look at how the *Alternate Perspectives* on your Persona respect and/or care for the non-human/non-user

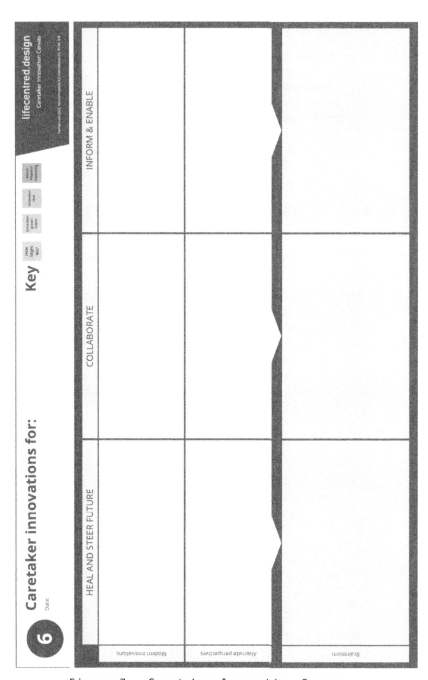

Figure 7 - Caretaker Innovation Canvas

2. Brainstorm innovations

Brainstorm innovations to fix your lifecycle and to ensure the ongoing thriving of your non-humans/non-users.

Drawing from your research, brainstorm how you can incorporate any solutions or devise your own and capture in the *Brainstorm* row of the **Product Lifecycle Innovation Canvas.**

You can also refer to circular lifecycle strategies:

- Optimise the use and life of the product:
  - o Make more durable
  - o Design for modularity and disassembly to enable easy repair and recycling
  - o Ensure your product uses energy efficiently

- Switch to more sustainable and ethical materials:
  - o Biodegradable, recycled, and recyclable materials
  - o Non-toxic and chemical free materials
  - o Materials that do not originate from areas known for conflict materials, forced labour, etc.
  - o Consider if any new materials you choose can deliver the same benefits as the materials you are replacing (such as durability, water resistance, etc.)

- Reduce the amount of materials, and the number of materials, by using ones that can be reused throughout the design
- Reduce or reuse any waste as a resource:
  - o Find uses for your waste either for your lifecycle or for use by other businesses or systems

- Design for post-use loops:
  - o Enable or invest in collection, repair, refurbishing, resell, repurpose, and recycling

- Foster user stewardship
  - o Inform users of sustainable behaviours and make it easier for them to choose these behaviours over others

Lifecycle Innovation

Next, use the **Caretaker Innovation Canvas** and draw from your research to brainstorm how the business can support the non-human/non-user beyond fixing damage.

Consider where the business can use its resources and prosperity to be an ongoing caretaker for the non-human/non-user, and its supporting actants, by conserving and nurturing their needs:

- **Heal past and steer future**—How can the non-human/non-user be healed, and protected from future damage and threats, for example:

  o **Support grass root causes** fighting for policy change by sharing and donating to their work
  o **Invest** in the regenerative futures of your industry, such as investing in the development of related lifecycle innovations and technologies

- **Collaborate and share**, for example

  o **Collaborate** with other businesses with the same non-human/non-user to share value, knowledge, and resources to collectively improve the relationship with the non-human/non-user
  o **Donate** to the local and/or global *Supportive Initiatives*, and to organisations that support the related SDGs

- **Inform and enable**—Connect users and the public with the non-humans/non-users, for example:

  o Identify user behaviours that may help reduce their impact, nurture the non-humans/non-users, and nurture the users relationship with them, while still allowing them to get what they need. For example:

    ▪ Volunteering initiatives such as litter clean-up days
    ▪ Donating to the *Supportive Initiatives*
    ▪ Reporting neglect or abuse of the non-human/non-user

110

- Raise user and the public awareness and educate them about the non-human/non-user's importance and needs, and highlight any needs they have in common with humans
- Inform users and the public of the activities and actions they can choose to support the non-humans/non-users—use your personas and artefacts to engage them
- Enable these activities and actions through promotions or organising events
- Encourage recurring engagement by giving users/citizens feedback on the impact of their actions and through sharing your own impacts

Caretaker Innovation

3. Refine ideas

By now you should have a lot of ideas.

Do a sense check for any that might obviously impact the Human needs (on your persona) in a negative way and consider removing these at this point.

Then use the **Innovation Refining Canvas** to refine the ideas into Innovation Statements.

1. In the *Refine Ideas* section on the canvas, collate all the ideas from both the **Lifecycle Innovation Canvas** and **Caretaker Innovation Canvas**
2. Cluster similar ideas, tease out detail, and refine the main ideas
3. In the *Innovation Statements* section, summarise your final ideas as statements about what they are, what problem they address, and how

111

Refining Innovations

4. Prioritise

- Use the **Priority Grid** to assess your innovation ideas for their feasibility and impact on the non-human/non-user
- Items in the top right are the most feasible and impactful. To prioritise these further, you can consider which innovations support any common needs of the non-human/non-user and humans
- Remember:
  - Just as there are trade-offs between the user and business needs, there will also be trade-offs between life-centred innovations and business needs as the world transitions to a less human-centred paradigm. But engaging in life-centred design is a commitment to push these business-as-usual boundaries, and to not be afraid of forsaking or using some profit to support and be a part of this transition
  - You may need to set up dual innovation streams, such as having one stream of small and quick wins, and another stream of work slowly evolving larger changes in the business model and/or system
  - The less certain you are about the impacts of a design decision, the smaller/simpler the version of the change you should make. You can always scale up after testing.

Making a physical service kinder

The method for making a physical service kinder is the same as above but using the **Service Lifecycle Innovation Canvas** instead to also research/brainstorm innovations for the service activities.

112

7. Support from the digital world

Humbled by your deeper connection with nature, you feel gratitude for what you take and more conscious that you give back more and only what is not harmful.

Pulling you from the moment, your device vibrates in your pocket, and you take it out to see several missed messages and notifications. Instead of immediately responding like you normally would, however, you remain present and calm, aware of how the device in your hand was made from the raw earth, from many different materials extracted and remixed and shipped to arrive reconfigured as technology for the convenience of yourself and millions of others.

More conscious of how deeply technology and its virtual world are embedded in the real-world, and their impacts, you realise you can change your own use of it in ways that better respect the needs of nature and its lifeforms.

Summary

Applying a digital lens, you'll explore which innovations you can support in your digital channels and how you can change user behaviour.

Time: 1-2 hrs

Method Tools: Digital Behaviour Solutions Canvas, Digital Journey Solutions Canvas

Design Modes: Brainstorming for Digital Design

Steps:

1. Brainstorm user behaviour solutions for each innovation using the **Digital Behaviour Solutions Canvas**
2. Use the **Digital Journey Solutions Canvas** to innovate digital journeys and to map new ones

Expert Steps:

- Use participatory design
- Share with experts or a coalition for feedback

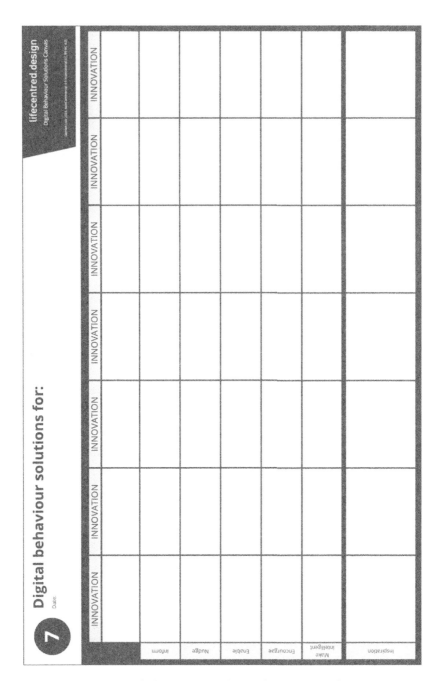

Figure 8 - Digital Behaviour Solutions Canvas

114

1. Innovate user behaviour solutions

Add your innovations onto the Digital Behaviour Solutions Canvas, on in each column.

Now you have innovations to support through digital, bring your thinking to the digital experience level and define digital solutions to support the innovations.

Using the **Digital Behaviour Solutions Canvas**, copy and paste each innovation into a square in the innovation row. Use multiple Canvasses if you need to.

Use the prompts to brainstorm digital solutions for each innovation

For each innovation, work your way down the page and use the prompts in the left-hand column to brainstorm digital solutions.

Research existing journey solutions and add to the inspiration columns for reference.

Determine behaviours—Determine behaviours and actions online and in the real-world that can be nudged such as donating, recycling, etc. to support your innovations.

Inform—Improve user awareness about the non-human/non-user and about their behaviour options:

- **Onboarding**—Introduce users to how your experience is supporting the non-humans/non-users with an engaging onboarding experience. To avoid overwhelming them with too much information, try progressive onboarding, revealing smaller pieces of information at different times
- **Informative content**—Provide helpful resources, such as creating a simple library of educational content and practical help such as tips and tools to enable users to be more involved
- **User content**—Publish user stories of how they have taken sustainable actions and the outcomes, or enable users to publish and share themselves
- **Non-human/non-user copy**—Infuse web copy with reference to non-humans/non-users, 'deepening the conversation and intent on the website' and increasing user awareness
- **Storytelling**—Use compelling narratives and visual storytelling (infographics, videos, and interactive) that resonate emotionally with users to emphasize the positive impact of sustainable choices
- **Connect to other resources**—Link to information to change users thinking and behaviours, such as provide links to helpful information

related to your non-human/non-user to raise user awareness and if possible nudge user behaviours that support them

Enable—Design digital solutions that allow users to change their behaviours:

- **Content hierarchy**—Use priority placement and visual hierarchy to make sustainable options easier to find and choose
- **Non-human/non-user copy**—Give voice to the non-human/non-user in the digital journey and communications with first-person voice messages, thanking users for sustainable choices and giving feedback on their impacts
- **Recommendations**—Recommend eco-friendly, durable, and sustainable options
- **Colour psychology**—Use calm colours and messaging (instead of time-based and urgent messaging such as 'Buy now' or 'Low stock') to help users slow down and make time for sustainable decision making
- **Tips**—Display Tips of the Day/Week to keep sustainability and responsible behaviours at the forefront of users' minds
- **Notifications and Reminders**:

  o Periodically educate users about the importance of reducing waste and provide actionable steps they can take
  o Inform about local events, repair workshops, or trade-in promotions, etc. happening in the user's area
  o Leverage user data to offer personalized behaviour, action, and post-purchase suggestions

- **Filtering**—Provide filtering for planet-friendly options, such as designing a 'planet-friendly' filter into catalogues and search results to allow users to easily identify more planet-friendly options that don't impact your related non-human/non-user (or impact them less), such as filtering locally-made, organic, and sustainable options
- **Connect to *Supportive initiatives***—Link to supporters, such as promoting and integrating not-for-profit and environmental organisations related to your non-human/non-user to nurture awareness and behavioural change, such as integrating registration and donation forms and linking to community events
- **Locators**—Incorporate a feature that helps users locate nearby organisations to assist in their sustainable behaviours, such as recycling centres, etc.
- **Calculator**—Integrate a calculator that estimates the carbon footprint associated with a user's behaviours

- **Guides and tutorials**—Integrate user-friendly, interactive instructional guides and tutorials, such as repair guides. Include detailed instructions, images, and videos to empower users
- **AR/VR/MR**—Provide augmented or virtual reality guides, tutorials, games to sustainable user behaviours, such as how they can repair their products, etc.

Encourage—Encourage repeatable action:

- **Forum**—Foster a sense of community and motivate others to participate by designing a community forum where users to allow users to share their success stories, tips, and challenges. Make it social by enabling user to inspire and learn from one another
- **Gamified learning**—Create interactive challenges, educational mini-games, or missions that encourage users to adopt sustainable behaviours
- **Rewards**—Reward users with points or virtual badges
- **Visual rewards**—Incorporate micro interactions to provide feedback and rewards when users take sustainable actions. For example, trigger a celebratory animation when they take a sustainable action
- **Feedback**—Display engaging visualizations and statistics that show users the positive impact and progress of their actions, perhaps create a personalised dashboard
- **Proof**—Display proof of any sustainable/quality/etc. claims, such as certifications, social proof, etc.

Make intelligent—Use data & metrics to personalise, give feedback, and monitor for progress

- **Reuse data differently**—Can any existing data be used differently to connect the experience and user with the initiatives, or to encourage user behaviour change?
- **Expand data sets**—Can any new data be sourced via the system (business 3rd parties, users, user 3rd parties, etc.) to help monitor the non-humans/non-users or user behaviour? Enable users to safely share their own data, or data they collect
- **User collected/shared data**—Can users share localised information regarding the non-human/non-user?
- **Data for metrics**—What metrics can you use to measure the positive or negative impact on the non-user of your design decisions?
- **AI**—Explore what AI tools can be incorporated

Research how other digital experiences may have solved the challenges and place them in the *Inspiration* row for reference.

Figure 9 - Digital Journey Solution Canvas

2. Innovate journeys

Use the **Digital Journey Solutions Canvas** to innovate your existing digital user journeys and to map new ones.

Review existing journeys

- Layout existing journeys in the *Screens* row
- Explore how you can implement the solutions from the **Digital Behaviour Solutions Canvas**

Map new journeys

- Using the *Innovation Statements* as prompts, research how other digital experiences may have solved the challenges and place them in the *Inspiration* row for reference
- Map any new journeys in the *Screens* row
- Explore how you can also implement any solutions from the **Digital Behaviour Solutions Canvas**

For all your digital solutions, refer to Sustainable Web Design strategies to design them in ways that minimise the energy they use.

Behaviour Solutions

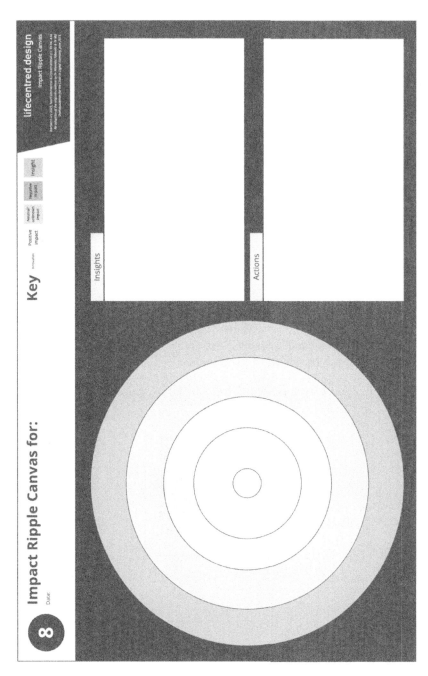

Figure 10 - Impact Ripple Canvas

8. Test from the futures

As you stroll by a river, with your new sense of presence and interconnectedness, the 'now' seems more vivid, alive, and playful.

You pick up a river pebble and throw it to skip it across the river's surface, each bounce causing ripples that glisten in the sunlight.

Your sense of interconnectedness, too, reaches out, to those who have lived before you, and to those yet to be born who will arrive in a world you leave for them.

Summary

Applying futures thinking, you'll aim to minimise unintended and potentially harmful consequences of your proposed innovations by speculating how their impacts might ripple out into the future.

Time: 10-30 mins

Method Tools: Impact Ripple Canvas

Design Modes: Speculating

Key steps:

1. Brainstorm impacts of your innovations
2. Analyse your ideas and summarise into key insights
3. Determine actions to address the insights

Expert Steps:

- Use participatory design
- Share with experts or a coalition for feedback

1. Brainstorm impacts of your innovations

The **Impact Ripple Canvas** was created by Dr Manuela Taboada & Dr Md Shahiduzzaman for exploring the unseen and unintended consequences of an action, decision, behaviour, trend, etc.

- Write your Persona's name in the centre circle of the canvas
- Write all your design innovations on stickies and place them in the first ripple around the Persona's name
- Brainstorm direct impacts of each innovation in the second ripple (and use a connecting line to show their connections)
- In the same ripple, brainstorm combined impacts of 2 or more innovations—use connecting lines again to show which innovations combine to cause the impact
- In the third ripple, repeat the method to brainstorm more indirect consequences of combined impacts
- Extend into new ripples of indirect and/or combined results as many times as desired
- Finish by brainstorming wider-reaching consequences by using the STEEPLE framework:

  - Society—How might human behaviours and societies change? How might minorities and the vulnerable be impacted?
  - Technology—What new technology might arise, or be abandoned, or how might they be used differently?
  - Environment—What greater environmental impact could this have?
  - Economic—How will spending habits change and what economies might be affected?
  - Politics—What power shifts may occur, and how might this affect freedoms, economies, etc?
  - Ethical—How will this change social responsibility in businesses, communities, and nations?

Example

To care for your 'Land' persona, you develop a 'collect and recycle' scheme for your product to reduce landfill. Customers love this and sales increase 500%. But you didn't reduce the use of new raw materials in your product, so the increased sales also increase the extraction of these materials which cause more harm to the land.

2. Analyse your ideas and summarise into key insights

- Gather all the ideas into the *Insights* box
- Cluster them into themes
- Write a summary of each theme as a Key Insight
- Ask yourself, do any of these insights have the potential to hurt the non-human/non-user's needs, enable their threats, or hurt human needs?

3. Determine actions to address the insights

- In the *Actions* box, define any new actions or changes required to address the *Insights* and implement as needed

Ripple Canvas1

9. Summarise with a vision

Returning from your future thinking to the 'now', you craft a preferred future vision to retain the experience your journey has given you, so that it may ripple out to others and inspire a greater sense of presence and connection between all peoples, and between people and the land.

Summary

Compile all your refined innovations into a summary to communicate the vision to your team and beyond.

The process of creating a summary helps you synthesise your statements into one cohesive and regenerative solution.

As well as a usual summary document, look to produce a creative visual summary. Allow this artefact to become a little forward thinking to show your vision beyond what may be immediately viable, yet still realistic in the sense of what *could* be achieved in the near future with more dedicated life-centred action and funding. You can use the **Impact Ripple Canvas** to explore future impacts to 'futurise' the vision, and use AI 'text to image' tools to create visuals. For example:

- **Future web page**
- **Future Headlines**, fictional news headlines representing the positive impacts of your improved product or service on the world and your non-human/non-user
- **Before and After visuals**, of your lifecycle and/or non human/non-user
- **Storyboard**, such as 'A Day in the Life" of your future users, non-humans/non-user
- **Short video**, such as a future commercial or documentary of your improved product or business
- **Social Media** stories, reels, or slideshows

Future Web Page

124

10. Stay with them

Before you head back to your design studio, you gaze over the landscape one more time, seeing the world differently now as a living, breathing, interconnected flow of energy and life.

You understand and feel how everything you create must be a symbiotic part of the ecosystem, and that your creations come with a responsibility to ensure they remain so.

Summary

To fully shift from being just a sustainable producer to also being an ongoing regenerative caretaker, determine metrics to measure your innovations' impact on the non-humans/non-users. Embed them and your insights into your handover documents to ensure they are not forgotten or deprioritised after they leave your safe hands, and so you can monitor them in the future.

Time: NA

Method Tools: Any of your completed canvases and work that will help communicate the importance of the innovations, and create empathy in the team (e.g., your Personas, multi-media persona artefacts, Lifecycle Maps, Visual Summary, etc.)

Design Modes: Compiling, Sharing, and Monitoring

Key steps:

1. Determine metrics
2. Embed personas and their needs into handover documentation
3. Keep personas updated

Expert Steps:

- Explore forming an alliance between other organisations, from your industry and others, who share the same non-humans/non-users to create a library of ideas and to learn from and inspire each other
- Keep your experts/coalition involved by sharing with them any post-launch success and failures

1. Determine metrics

What would be the signs of success for your innovations and how can you measure and monitor them?

- What *existing* data could be used to measure the non-human/non-user's health, responses, behaviours, etc. related to your innovations?
- What *new* data could be used?
- How can you collect that data? What existing or new tech in your product/service can be used to capture and/or monitor data to give non-humans/non-users a voice?
- For animals interacting with your lifecycle, can you safely and ethically employ Animal-Computer Interaction systems that can also be used for tracking, such as:
  - o Screen and Tracking Systems
  - o Haptic and Wearable Systems
  - o Tangible and Physical Systems
- Set up a cadence to check data post-launch and assess for impacts to the persona needs
- How will you hold yourself accountable for these solutions? For example, posting commitments on the website and updating progress/metrics

2. Embed non-humans/non-users and their needs in design handover

- Present the **Personas**, other **artefacts**, **Lifecycle Maps** and **Visual Summary** to the wider team, highlighting the design decisions made for the non-humans/non-users and the reasoning
- Embed **Personas**, metrics, etc. into design handover documentation
- Share multimedia persona artefacts to help business empathise more deeply
- Be available to answer any questions
- Allow others to edit and add to the personas as learnings arise

3. Keep personas updated

Update and evolve the personas over time:

- Update personas as learnings arise and each time you check post-launch
- Allow new primary personas to be discovered
- Know when to let personas go—for example if you created a persona for water and you managed to remove all use of water and any impacts to it, you wouldn't need to refer to water's needs anymore in design/decision-making (unless there was still healing to be done)

Method 2 – Innovating digital things

Not every business has influence over how their products are made. Or, they may be a purely online experience that doesn't sell physical products or services. And while most businesses have a website, applying sustainable web design strategies will reveal and resolve the energy, accessibility, and inclusivity issues without the need for a persona.

However, a 'purely' digital experience, such as learning and social media platforms, can still use non-human/non-user personas to innovate life-centred change.

Firstly, a generalised Earth/Nature persona can be used to introduce the team and clients to non-human/non-user/life-centred thinking and to generate initial innovations and ideas for further exploration.

Secondly, specific non-humans/non-users can be identified for 'purely' digital experiences from two perspectives:

- Who are the non-humans/non-users impacted by *your product/business's industry* (e.g., the education industry, etc.)?
- Who are the non-humans/non-users impacted by the *digital technology industry*?

If we remember that non-human/non-user personas are best used to compliment broader innovation, they can be used to compliment sustainable web design strategies in two key ways:

- To innovate the business model, and/or
- To innovate the digital experience

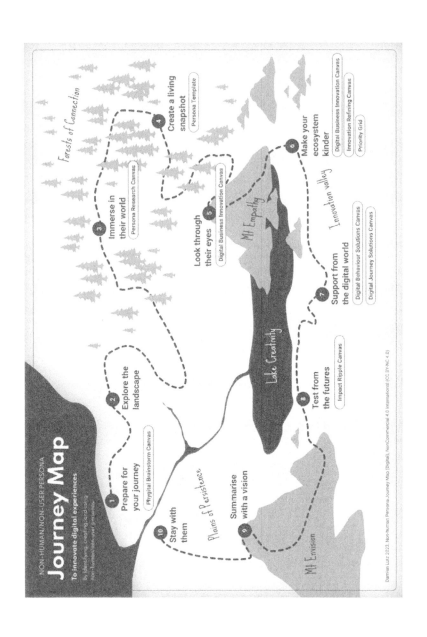

Figure 11 - Journey Map (Digital)

Method 2 Summary

1. **Prepare for your journey** by brainstorming the physical things that enable and support your digital experience

2. **Explore the landscape**—Determine the non-humans/non-users you'll focus on

3. **Immerse in their world**—Research your non-humans/non-users

4. **Create a living snapshot**—Synthesise your research into Personas and other artefacts

5. **Look through their eyes**—Apply the Personas as lenses to determine impacts to the non-human/non-users

6. **Make your experience kinder**—Brainstorm how the business can support the non-humans/non-users by supporting initiatives, innovating the business, and enabling kinder user/citizen behaviours

7. **Support from the digital world**—Support business and behaviour innovation ideas through the digital experience

8. **Test from the futures**—Explore potential future impacts of your innovations to reduce unintended consequences

9. **Summarise with a vision**—Create a visual summary to synthesise and share your regenerative vision

10. **Stay with them**—Determine metrics to measure the innovations' impact on the non-humans/non-users, embed their needs in your handover process, and evolve the personas over time

*Note: A **Time** is shown at each stage—this approximates how long it might take to complete just the Key Steps.*

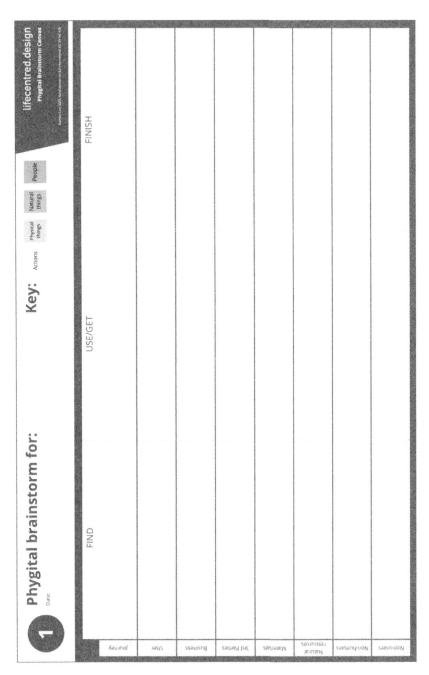

Figure 12 - Phygital Brainstorm Canvas

132

1. Prepare for your journey

You peer out over the vast landscape awaiting your exploration, humbled by nature's complex balance and excited by what you'll see and learn.

Summary

To prepare your mindset, you'll brainstorm the physical things that support your digital experience.

Time: 20 mins

Persona Tools: Phygital Map

Steps:

1. Brainstorm the physical things supporting the digital experience and the non-users and non-humans impacted
2. Pause and reflect

This is meant to be a fast and simple brainstorming exercise without any research, purely to open your mind to the scope of physical things that support your digital experience, and the impacts they might have. Set yourself a timer for 1 or 2 minutes per row.

1. Map the phygital

Using the Phygital Brainstorm Canvas, follow the prompts to explore the physical roots and impacts of your digital experience.

1. *Map a simple user journey*—Brainstorm the main user journey of your digital experience. Keep it high level, using the headings as a guide (e.g., User web searches for your service, user lands on your home page, user searches for a product, user purchases product, user receives confirmation email).

2. *Brainstorm the physical things a user needs*—Brainstorm the *minimal* physical things a user needs to complete these tasks (e.g., device, internet connection)

3. *Brainstorm the physical things the business needs to enable the user experience*—Brainstorm the *main* physical things and services your business needs to provide the user experience (e.g., computers, servers, internet connection, web hosting)

4. *Brainstorm the physical things any 3rd Parties needs to support the business*—Brainstorm the 3rd parties that provide any services, then brainstorm the physical things they need (e.g., computers, servers, internet connection)

5. *Brainstorm the materials*—Brainstorm the materials required for all the physical things (e.g., plastic, glass, and metals for devices)

6. *Brainstorm the natural resources needed*—Brainstorm the natural resources used to make materials and products (e.g., silicon for glass, oil for plastic, oil for energy, etc.)

7. *Brainstorm the non-users impacted*—Brainstorm the environments where these materials are extracted and how they are impacted (e.g., land and soil is disturbed, wildlife habitat destroyed, water ways polluted, etc.)

8. *Brainstorm the non-humans impacted*—Brainstorm the humans impacted by the processes that extract the materials and manufacture the physical things

Phygital Canvas

134

2. Pause and reflect

When you're done, sit back and consider the scope of physical things required to enable and support your digital experience, how their roots reach down into the earth and human life.

2. Explore the landscape

Hitching your backpack over your shoulders, you explore the landscape to map its complexities and learn about its lifeforms and their interconnectedness.

Summary

You'll determine the non-humans/non-users you'll focus on by considering those impacted the digital tech industry.

Time: 10-20 mins

Method Tools: None

Design Modes: Decision-making

Choose your non-humans/non-users

While all digital experiences have real-world impacts due to the physical resources they use, such as servers, computers, devices, internet networks, etc., most digital businesses don't have direct influence over transitioning this technology to be more sustainable.

However, they can *support existing regenerative and sustainable initiatives*, and *encourage sustainable user behaviour*, using personas for the main non-humans/non-users that the technology industry impact.

Choose one you might do the least for, have the most influence over, or which calls to you the most:

- Non-humans impacted by the tech industry—Air, land, soil, water systems, forests, and climate for the impact from mining, production, and e-waste
- Non-users impacted by the tech industry—Forced labourers, child labourers, unsafe/underpaid labourers, and local and indigenous communities impacted by mines, factories, and waste/landfill areas

Review your Phygital canvas for any other non-humans/non-users you may have thought of.

You can also research to learn about specific places, animals, and people you could create personas for. Note that what you learn may get uncomfortable, such as the stories of children mining in the brutal artisanal mines in Congo—use your discomfort as a gauge to know you have delved deep enough to learn new things.

Example

Social media platforms are great drivers of the use of digital technology, and therefore contribute to major problems such as e-waste.

What if the Instagram team created a 'non-living' non-human persona for e-waste to understand it more as a world actant—its importance, how it's created, its lifecycles and impacts, etc. The persona could speak from the perspective that it wants to live longer through repair, resale, and recycling. Its challenges would be barriers to these needs, such as the inconvenience of recycling locations. The team could then use the persona to innovate how the business could directly support local and global initiatives while also enabling sustainable user behaviour to reduce e-waste.

For example, if Instagram can detect a user's device, they could estimate when the user may be looking to upgrade to know when to display helpful adverts or notifications that inform the user about local re-sell and recycle locations and services. Instagram could partner with these services to develop collection services in key areas to address the barrier of inconvenience.

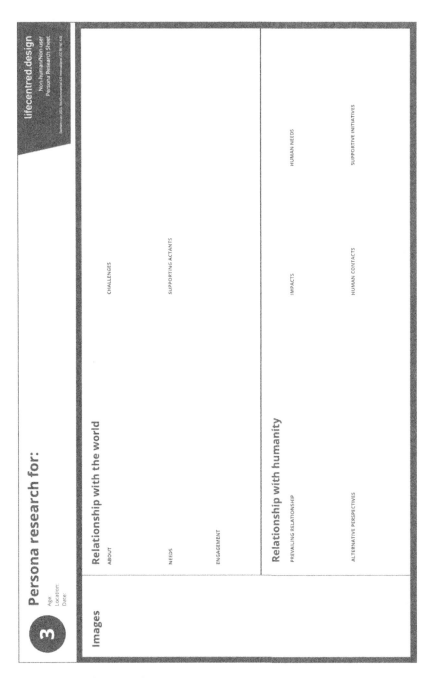

Figure 13 - Persona Research Canvas

3. Immerse in their world

Having spotted various lifeforms in the wild and identified those in need, you immerse yourself in their world to understand what challenges them and what makes them thrive.

Summary

You'll collect fact-based insights about your primary non-humans/non-users through research to document their place in the world, their importance, their needs and threats, and their relationship with humanity.

Time: 1-2 hrs per persona

Method Tools: Persona Research Canvas

Design Modes: Research

Key Steps:

1. Research facts
2. Pause and reflect

Expert Steps:

- Interview experts
- Form a coalition
- If given consent, study any human non-user in their environment
- If legally and safely possible, study any animal in their environment:

  o What do their behaviours tell you is important to them?
  o How does the environment treat them back?
  o If your non-human is a domestic animal, and you have legal and safe access to them, allow them to initiate and lead play and follow their lead to explore how that interaction is different from the usual experience of human-led interaction

1. Research facts

Follow the **Research Guide** for best practices, research to collect fact-based information about your non-humans/non-users on the **Persona Research Canvas**.

Below are suggestions about what information to research, based on insights from the practitioners and experiments shared earlier in this book. Feel free to include anything else that could inform design decisions specific to your project.

Collect lots of interesting bits of information, as you'll make sense of it all later. Follow tangents and immerse yourself in learning about the non-human/non-user—this researching process is as important as creating the persona.

How deep your research goes is up to you, but you need at least enough detail to understand the non-human/nonuser's needs.

Be prepared for unexpected and/or uncomfortable emotions arising as you delve into the lives of people, plants, animals, and environments—how humanity might be treating them in terrible ways, and how your own behaviours may play a contributing role. Use this discomfort as a measure that you are going deep enough in your research to ensure you are not just identifying key needs but also getting the key benefit from creating personas—empathy. Let these emotions come up, knowing that you will harness them and their energy in positive ways in *Stage 6 – Make your ecosystem kinder*.

In fact, as you do this research, you'll most likely discover more kind and healing innovations, so note them down to come back to later.

Note: Identifying and defining personas can be iterative throughout the process. Be open to adding and pivoting to any new non-human/non-users that arise at any stage.

Start researching

Identification data

Give the persona a name, and for non-users (being humans), also give them a descriptor, such as 'Factory worker'.

Collect:

- Images—Web search or try a resource like *unsplash.com* to find a key image that:
    - Is instantly recognisable
    - Captures the non-human's importance 'in action'
    - Conveys some emotion

140

- Age and lifespan
- Habitat locations specific to your persona, but also add where else they can be found (e.g., the River Systems in the example Persona was based in Australia, but they are found worldwide)

Relationship with the world

- **About, Needs, and Engagement**
  - **About**
    - For non-users, gather facts and scenarios to feed into a general definition and summary of what they do, their role in the world and in the business ecosystem, and some history, quality of life, attitudes, interests, hopes, statistics, etc. Consider also if their way of existing is different to yours. For example, do they work according to the Gregorian calendar or lunar cycles (or both); do they follow any cultural cycles?
    - For non-humans, what does the non-human/non-user do for the world and why is this important? Are they part of a greater system/cycle? What other lifeforms or cycles rely on the non-human/non-user for their own healthy existence? Include key statistics. Consider what cycles they might synchronise with—for example, if they're an animal, are they diurnal or nocturnal, etc.?
  - **Needs**—What do they need to survive and thrive (e.g., food, habitat, room for roaming or migration, etc.) If you can determine with factual evidence, include their needs for beyond basic needs to survive, such as what is known to give them joy
  - **Engagement**—How do they interact with the world?
    - Communication—How do they communicate? (e.g., plant roots use fungi to communicate with each other, and bees use dance and vibration to communicate, human workers might use Whatsapp)
    - Interaction—For animals, what are their forms of interaction with world? (e.g., dogs bite to pull, monkeys climb with arms and legs, etc.). For humans, do they have any unique forms of interaction? (e.g., A blind or visually impaired person uses sound and tactile interaction methods). Plants *filter* gases (carbon and oxygen) and nutrients, rivers *move* and *pulse*.
    - Navigation—For animals, how do they sense and navigate environments (e.g., bats use sonar), and how do these abilities change with different environments? For humans, do they have

any unique forms of navigation? (e.g., A blind or visually impaired person might use a cane, service animal, and GPS)

- Additional Engagement research for animal non-humans—If you are designing something for an animal to interact with, these are research questions to learn more about their behaviours and interactions:
  - How do animals complete the same or similar tasks to humans?
  - What are the animal's types of interaction, and which are most common (e.g., noise, licking, touching, brushing against others, electromagnetic, etc.)
  - What elicits different types of responses?
  - How do they communicate with each other and with lifeforms outside their specie?
  - What are their mental skills (learning, recall, solving problems, etc.)?
  - What are their routines and rituals?
  - What's a day in their life?

- **Challenges and Supporting Actants**

  - **Challenges**—What threatens their ability to obtain food and shelter, to procreate, to be valued, or to do what they need to do that makes them important in the world?
  - **Supporting Actants**—Who are the key actants that the non-human/non-user relies on for a healthy existence? Who or what enables the non-human/non-user's food, habitat, room for roaming/migration, procreation, etc? (e.g., birds need worms for food, flowers need bees to pollinate them). What are the supporters' key needs to thrive? (If any of these are significant in any way, such as essential for the survival of the primary non-human/non-user or in critical danger, you might want to make a persona for them also).

Relationship with humanity

- **Prevailing relationship and impacts**

  - What is the dominant human relationship with the non-human/non-user that has the most power over it? What is the nature of this relationship?

    - For environments and animals—Do humans engage, use, harm, nurture, and/or exclude the non-human/non-user? How important does humanity view and treat them? (e.g., humans in developing countries often disrespect their unused electronics by not re-using them but discarding them as e-waste)

- For human non-users—What is their status in society's eyes, how are they treated, included, or excluded, etc.?; What are their privileges or lack of?

o Impacts—What are the impacts of the prevailing relationship on the non-humans/non-users?

- **Alternate perspectives, Human contacts, and Supportive initiatives**

  o **Alternate perspectives**—What are less common human relationships with the non-human/non-user? Often dominance over environments and animals belongs to Euro-Western, capitalistic, development-focused peoples. If this is the case for your non-humans/non-users, what are alternate perspectives and relationships that are better for the health of their world and can be explored to improve the damaging relationships:

    - For environments and animals—How are they respected and nurtured, and who does this well? (e.g., Ghanaians working in the dump sites of e-waste sent from other countries value the e-waste as income by sorting and reselling it)
    - For human non-users—Do they have unappreciated and/or untapped value? (e.g., not just a factory worker but a world citizen deserving of foundational rights and respect). How do different organisations treat or support them?

  o **Human contacts**—Consider who most engages with your non-human/non-user:

    - Examples of key human contacts for non-humans—Farmer, Animal Welfare Officer, Consumer, Captive parent, Pet parent, Hunter
    - Examples of key human contacts for non-users—Boss, Delivery drivers, Support groups, Parole officer, Doctor, Neighbour

  o **Supportive Initiatives**

    - What are the organisations and initiatives that support the non-humans/non-users? Are there local, national, and global initiatives?
    - The United Nations Sustainable Development Goals (SDGs) are 17 interconnected global goals created by the United Nations that form 'a shared blueprint for peace and prosperity for people and

the planet (see *https://sdgs.un.org/goals*). What SDGs are the non-human/non-user related to?

Persona Research

2. Pause and reflect

- When you feel you're done, take a short break, and then come back to your work
- Ask yourself if there is anything missing or needs clarifying
- Gather any further research you feel is required

When you feel your research is complete, take another well-earned break, or jump into bringing your non-humans/non-users to life by compiling your research into persona documents and other artefacts.

4. Create a living snapshot

After your deep exploration of the lifeforms most in need, you take a seat on a log atop a valley edge, gaze over the landscape, and create a mental snapshot so you don't forget what you've learned about them and their needs.

Summary

Informed by your research, you'll now create the persona—a 'living snapshot' of your non-human/non-user—by synthesising your research into succinct personas that are effective for communicating the non-human/non-user's needs and perspectives during decision-making.

Time: 30-60 mins per persona

Method Tools: Persona Template

Design Modes: Synthesising and Persona Creation

Key Steps:

    A. Choose how to best represent the non-human/non-user

    B. Synthesise your research onto the **Persona Template**

    C. Explore the need for other persona artefacts

Expert Steps:

- Co-create with the business
- Interview experts
- Share with a coalition for feedback

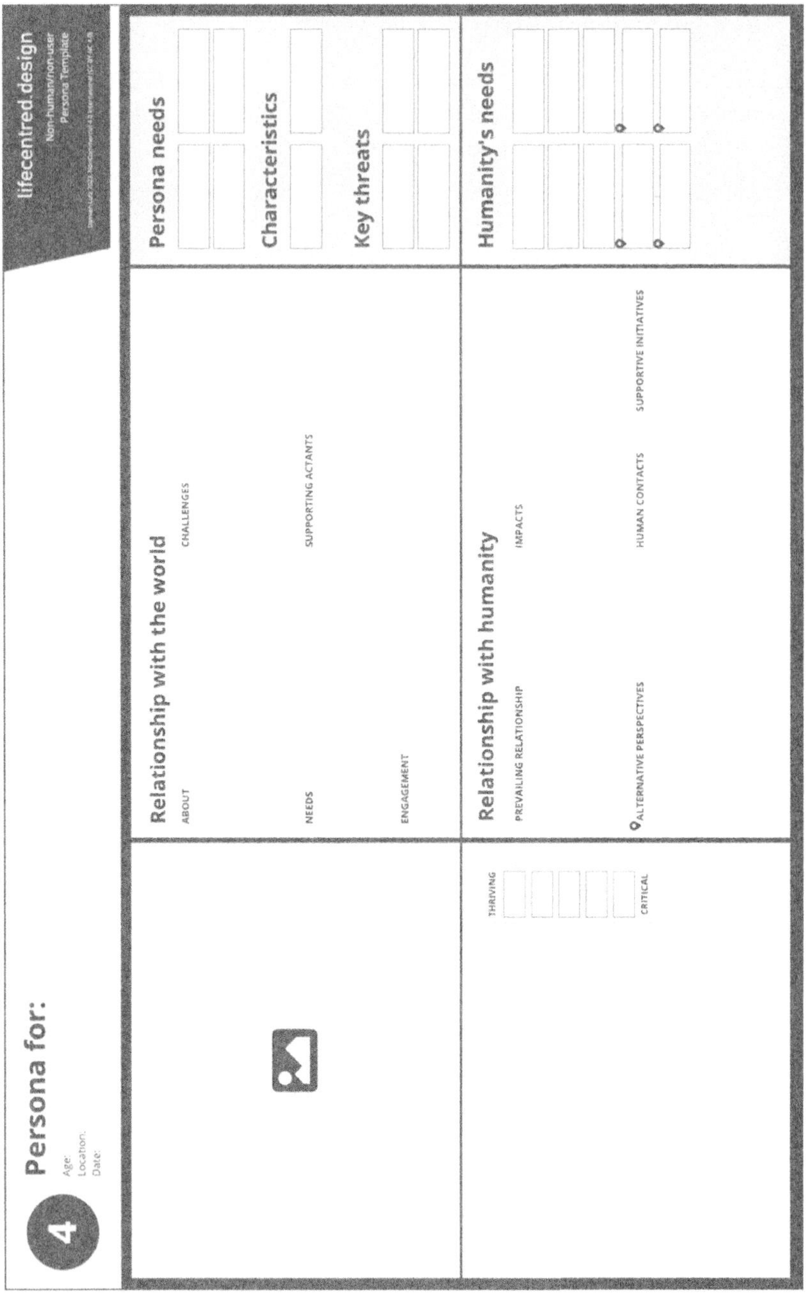

Figure 14 - Persona Template

1. Choose the best representation

If you haven't already, decide how the non-human/non-user would best be represented:

- Individual—For a specific individual non-human/non-user
- Group—A herd/flock/etc., family, community, minority group, etc.
- Specie

2. Synthesise your research onto the Persona Template

Create 'a source of truth' persona for each non-human/non-user, one that is easily edited, readable, and sharable for feedback and collaboration.

This source of truth can then be used to create different persona artefacts in different mediums based on a project's needs (more about that later).

About the Persona Template

The template consists of five sections:

A. Identity Header
B. Empathy summary (left-hand column)
C. Relationship with the world row
D. Relationship with humanity row
E. The Needs and Threats column

1. Identity Header

Name your persona, capture its locations and age, and add the date you're creating the persona.

2. Empathy Summary

The empathy section consists of a key image, a written summary, and a health rating, with the purpose being to generate empathy for the non-human/non-user without designers and workshop participants reading all the detail.

Image

Web search or try a resource like *unsplash.com* to find a key image that:
- Is instantly recognisable
- Captures the non-human's importance 'in action'
- Conveys some emotion

Written Summary

The written summary can be read at design and decision-making times to aid in remembering and *feeling* the non-human/non-user's needs.

It can be written in first person, as if the non-human/non-user is speaking, to help readers empathise—avoid over-humanising by using language that reflects their values and world. Or it can be written from an observer's perspective to ensure readers understand the persona is an outside perspective.

Health Rating

Estimate the non-human/non-user's current health rating on a rating from critical to thriving. You can use colour for emphasis and arrows to show if they are improving or worsening.

- For animals and environments, consider the species' predicament in the world, if they are declining or thriving
- For human non-users consider the quality of their life, opportunities, and if these are improving or worsening

3. Relationship with the world

Importance and Challenges

Summarise how the non-human/non-user are important to the world, and what threatens their safety and longevity.

Needs and Supporting actants

Summarise their needs to survive and thrive, and what actants support their existence and how.

Engagement

Note how they engage with the world.

Non-human/non-user needs

In the right column, summarise your non-human/non-user insight into their key needs for surviving, healing, and thriving. Include key needs for their supporters.

Key threats

Summarise the challenges into the most serious threats to the non-human/non-user.

4. Relationship with humanity

Prevailing relationship and Impacts

Summarise who has the most power over the non-human/non-user and what their relationship is with them—do they support them, use them, what are their attitudes toward their value, and how are they impacted?

Alternative Perspectives

Summarise alternate perspectives and relationships with your non-human/non-user, such as the Supportive Initiatives and those with less control over the dominant relationships with the humans/non-users.

Human contacts

Reviewing your research, determine the main human contact(s) for your non-human/non-user. This is to identify who might be inspiration and/or allies in assisting with innovation. If you have several to choose from, prioritise who is most closely related to your non-human's relationship with your product lifecycle.

Supportive initiatives

Reviewing your research, determine who are the main group(s) that support your non-human/non-user. Include the related United Nations Sustainable Development Goals (SDG). Again, this is to identify who might be inspiration and/or allies in assisting with innovation.

Consider what's being done at all levels:

- Macro—Initiatives working at a global level
- Meso—Initiatives working at the local level, such as collaborations, local communities, etc.
- Micro—Initiatives by individuals

Humanity's needs

In the right column, summarise humanity's needs of the non-human.

For human non-user personas, summarise what humanity needs *to do* to make life better for the non-users.

Reflecting on the needs of the non-human/non-user, their supporters' needs, and humanity's needs, identify and highlight any that are common—these can be priority needs to focus on when designing.

E-waste Persona

150

3. Explore other artefacts

Different projects might require different persona artefacts, such as any research output that is specific for the project.

Also, multi-media versions such as video and audio can be powerful in emotionally engaging and influencing business, partners, and the public.

Determine if other artefacts might be useful for your project

Examples:

- Multi-media artefacts to engage and influence business, partners, and the public:
    - A video—this can be simple, such as one continuous shot or image with narration, or a story with sound effects
    - An audio of someone speaking in the first person of the non-human/non-user
    - A written short story

- Journey maps
    - A day/night in the life of your non-human/non-user
    - How and when humans interact with the non-human/non-user (e.g., farmer milking a cow, birdwatcher spying birds, scientists studying frogs in a stream, etc.)
    - The non-human/non-user's journey through history

- Design principles to guide micro-level design (UX, UI, etc.) and to share with other business areas such as marketing

See the **Persona Library** for examples of the above.

An Audio Persona

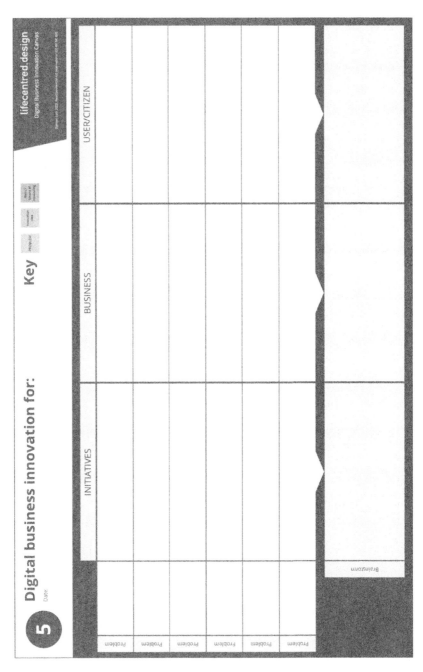

Figure 15 - Digital Business Innovation Canvas

5. Look through their eyes

You close your eyes for a moment, and imagine being one of the lifeforms you've discovered, their needs now your needs. You open your eyes again and see the landscape in an entirely new way as if looking through their eyes, heart, and mind.

Summary

Referring to your personas, and using the **Digital Business Innovation Canvas**, you'll determine the problems that need to be addressed and research for existing solutions.

Time: 1 hr

Method Tools: Your completed Personas, Digital Business Innovation Canvas

Design Modes: Research

Steps:

1. Empathise
2. Determine Problems
3. Research innovations

Expert Steps:

- Interview experts
- Share with a coalition for feedback
- Use participatory analysis

1. Empathise with the non-human/non-user

Before using the persona to assess the system for how it impacts them, use the *Empathise Summary* to connect and empathise with your non-human/non-user.

Read the *Empathy Summary* as a mediative approach by imagining being the persona, and their needs are your needs.

This immersive approach is meant to help de-centre yourself and critique the design with less bias and more from the non-human/non-user's perspective.

2. Determine problems

Using the **Digital Business Innovation Canvas,** collate findings from your persona research into problems.

A problem should be something that contributes to the issue related to the non-human. For example, for the non-human e-waste, problems are:

- Devices aren't used for as long as they could be
- Users aren't aware of recycling options
- Re-use, repair, and recycling options have barriers to use

Look at the persona needs and threats and write a problem statement for each one in a separate row on the canvas. You might group some into one statement, and you might need to use more than one canvas.

3. Research solutions

Research for existing solutions to the problems.

First look to your persona research—particularly the *Alternate perspectives,* *Supportive initiatives*, *Supporting actants*—and do any further research if you need.

- **Initiatives**—In this row, place any global, local, and independent organisations, activities, or initiatives that relate to each problem (e.g., International E-waste Day, SDG#12 Responsible consumption and production)
- **Business**—In this row, place any existing business-level activities that could support the non-human/non-user (e.g., product redesign, trade-in and buyback programs to ensure devices aren't dumped, etc.)
- **User/citizen**—In this row, place any user and citizen behaviours that could support the non-human/non-user (e.g., repair devices themselves, stop keeping old devices in draws at home and resell or recycle them, etc.) and initiatives that support them. Make note of any barriers to these behaviours, too

Digital Innovations

6. Make your ecosystem kinder

Infused with a deeper empathy, you seek ways to harmonise with nature, so that you become more life-centred and symbiotic with the world, take only what is needed, and regenerate the landscape and its lifeforms.

Summary

You'll now brainstorm how the business can support the non-humans/non-users by supporting initiatives, innovating the business, and enabling kinder user/citizen behaviours.

Time: 1-2 hrs

Method Tools: Digital Business Innovation Canvas, Innovation Refining Canvas, Priority Grid

Design Modes: Brainstorming, Insight synthesising

Steps:

1. Brainstorm innovations
2. Refine ideas
3. Prioritise

Expert Steps:

- Interview experts
- Share with a coalition for feedback
- Use participatory design

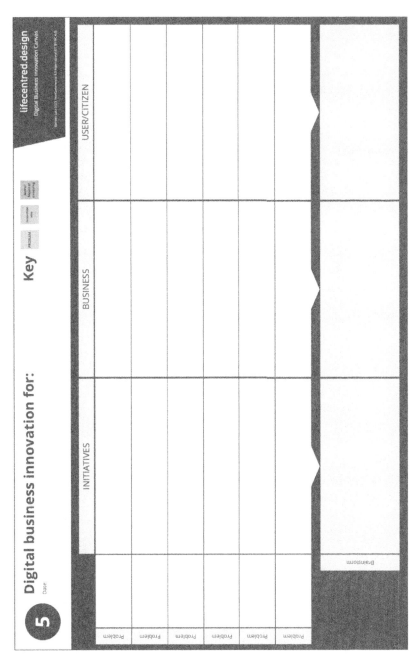

Figure 16 - Digital Business Innovation Canvas

1. Brainstorm innovations

Using the insight on your **Digital Business Innovation Canvas**, brainstorm in the bottom row how the business can support the non-human/non-user in such ways as:

- **Initiatives**—Donate, promote, or collaborate with initiatives enabling solutions now or developing long term solutions and technologies
- **Business innovation**—Innovate the business and/or collaborate with 'competitor' businesses to collectively improve the relationship with the non-human/non-user by sharing information, solutions, and resources
- **User/citizen behaviour**—Connect users and the public with the non-humans/non-users by informing and enabling supportive actions they can take:

  o Raise user and public awareness and educate them about the non-human/non-user's importance and needs, and highlight any needs they have in common with the non-humans/non-users
  o Inform users and the public of the activities and actions they can choose to support the non-humans/non-users—use your personas and artefacts to engage them
  o Enable these activities and actions through promotions or organising events
  o Encourage recurring engagement by giving users and the public feedback on the impact of their actions

Digital Innovations

3. Refine ideas

By now you should have a lot of innovation ideas.

Do a sense check for any ideas that might obviously impact the *Human needs* on your persona in a negative way and consider removing these at this point.

You might have some obvious quick wins, but for others that need further refinement or investigation:

1. Collate the ideas in the *Refine Ideas* section on the **Innovation Refining Canvas**.
2. Refine ideas by clustering similar ideas, tease out detail and refine the ideas
3. *Innovation Statements*—Summarise your final ideas as statements about what they are, what problem they address, and how

4. Prioritise

- Use the **Priority Grid** to assess innovation ideas for their feasibility and impact on the world
- Items in the top right are the most feasible and impactful. To prioritise these further, you can consider which innovations support the *Common Needs* (on the Persona)
- Remember:

  o Just as there are trade-offs between the user and business needs, there will also be trade-offs between life-centred innovations and business needs as the world transitions to a less human-centred paradigm. But engaging in life-centred design is a commitment to push these business-as-usual boundaries, and to not be afraid of forsaking or using some profit to support and be a part of this transition
  o You may need to set up dual innovation streams—You might have one stream of work slowing evolving larger changes in the business model and/or system, with a stream of smaller, faster quick wins

7. Support from the digital world

Humbled by your deeper connection with nature, you feel gratitude for what you take from it and more conscious that what you give back is more and regenerative and not harmful.

Your phone vibrates in your pocket, and you take it out to see several missed messages and notifications. Instead of immediately responding like you normally would, you feel more present now, and aware of how the device in your hand was made from the raw earth, many different materials extracted and remixed and shipped to arrive reconfigured as technology to you and millions of others.

More conscious of how deeply technology and its virtual world are embedded in the world, and its impact, you realise you can change your own use of it in ways that better respect the needs of nature and its lifeforms.

Summary

Now you have innovations to support through digital, bring your thinking to the digital experience level and define digital solutions to support the innovations.

Time: 1-2 hrs

Method Tools: Digital Behaviour Solutions Canvas, Digital Journey Solutions Canvas

Design Modes: Brainstorming for Digital Design

Steps:

1. Brainstorm user behaviour solutions to support your *Innovation Statements*
2. Innovate user journeys to support your *Innovation Statements*

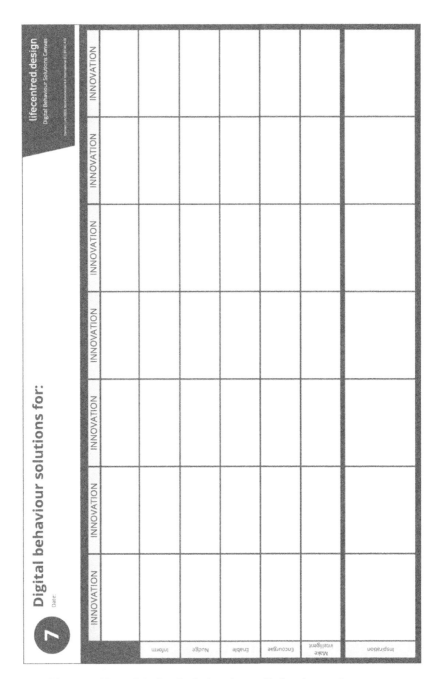

Figure 17 - Digital Behaviour Solutions Canvas

1. Innovate user behaviour

Add your *Innovation Statements* to the Digital Behaviour Solutions Canvas, placing one statement in each box under the Subject headings. Use multiple Canvasses if you need to.

For each statement, work your way down the page and use the prompts in the left-hand column to brainstorm digital solutions.

Research existing journey solutions and add to the inspiration columns for reference.

Inform—Improve user awareness about the non-human/non-user and about their behaviour options:

- **Onboarding**—Introduce users to how your experience is supporting the non-humans/non-users with an engaging onboarding experience. To avoid overwhelming them with too much information, try progressive onboarding, revealing smaller pieces of information at different times
- **Informative content**—Provide helpful resources, such as creating a simple library of educational content and practical help such as tips and tools to enable users to be more involved
- **User content**—Publish user stories of how they have taken sustainable actions and the outcomes, or enable users to publish and share themselves
- **Non-human/non-user copy**—Infuse web copy with reference to non-humans/non-users, 'deepening the conversation and intent on the website' and increasing user awareness
- **Storytelling**—Use compelling narratives and visual storytelling (infographics, videos, and interactive) that resonate emotionally with users to emphasize the positive impact of sustainable choices
- **Connect to other resources**—Link to information to change users thinking and behaviours, such as provide links to helpful information related to your non-human/non-user to raise user awareness and if possible nudge user behaviours that support them

Enable—Design digital solutions that allow users to change their behaviours:

- **Content hierarchy**—Use priority placement and visual hierarchy to make sustainable options easier to find and choose
- **Non-human/non-user copy** —Give voice to the non-human/non-user in the digital journey and communications with first-person voice messages, thanking users for sustainable choices and giving feedback on their impacts

- **Recommendations**—Recommend eco-friendly, durable, and sustainable options
- **Colour psychology**—Use calm colours and messaging (instead of time-based and urgent messaging such as 'Buy now' or 'Low stock') to help users slow down and make time for sustainable decision making
- **Tips**—Display Tips of the Day/Week to keep sustainability and responsible behaviours at the forefront of users' minds
- **Notifications and Reminders**:

  o Periodically educate users about the importance of reducing waste and provide actionable steps they can take
  o Inform about local events, repair workshops, or trade-in promotions, etc. happening in the user's area
  o Leverage user data to offer personalized behaviour, action, and post-purchase suggestions

- **Filtering**—Provide filtering for planet-friendly options, such as designing a 'planet-friendly' filter into catalogues and search results to allow users to easily identify more planet-friendly options that don't impact your related non-human/non-user (or impact them less), such as filtering locally-made, organic, and sustainable options
- **Connect to *Supportive initiatives***—Link to supporters, such as promoting and integrating not-for-profit and environmental organisations related to your non-human/non-user to nurture awareness and behavioural change, such as integrating registration and donation forms and linking to community events
- **Locators**—Incorporate a feature that helps users locate nearby organisations to assist in their sustainable behaviours, such as recycling centres, etc.
- **Calculator**—Integrate a calculator that estimates the carbon footprint associated with a user's behaviours
- **Guides and tutorials**—Integrate user-friendly, interactive instructional guides and tutorials, such as repair guides. Include detailed instructions, images, and videos to empower users
- **AR/VR/MR**—Provide augmented or virtual reality guides, tutorials, games to sustainable user behaviours, such as how they can repair their products, etc.

Encourage—Encourage repeatable action:

- **Forum**—Foster a sense of community and motivate others to participate by designing a community forum where users to allow users to share their success stories, tips, and challenges. Make it social by enabling user to inspire and learn from one another

- **Gamified learning**—Create interactive challenges, educational mini-games, or missions that encourage users to adopt sustainable behaviours
- **Rewards**—Reward users with points or virtual badges
- **Visual rewards**—Incorporate micro interactions to provide feedback and rewards when users take sustainable actions. For example, trigger a celebratory animation when they take a sustainable action
- **Feedback**—Display engaging visualizations and statistics that show users the positive impact and progress of their actions, perhaps create a personalised dashboard
- **Proof**—Display proof of any sustainable/quality/etc. claims, such as certifications, social proof, etc.

Make intelligent—Use data & metrics to personalise, give feedback, and monitor for progress

- **Reuse data differently**—Can any existing data be used differently to connect the experience and user with the initiatives, or to encourage user behaviour change?
- **Expand data sets**—Can any new data be sourced via the system (business 3rd parties, users, user 3rd parties, etc.) to help monitor the non-humans/non-users or user behaviour? Enable users to safely share their own data, or data they collect
- **User collected/shared data**—Can users share localised information regarding the non-human/non-user?
- **Data for metrics**—What metrics can you use to measure the positive or negative impact on the non-user of your design decisions?
- **AI**—Explore what AI tools can be incorporated

When you're done, review your digital experience journeys to determine where best to apply your digital innovations.

Behaviour Solutions

Figure 18 - Digital Journey Solution Canvas

2. Innovate journeys

Using the *Innovation Statements* as prompts, review your existing user journeys or design new ones to using the **Digital Journey Solutions Canvas.**

In the Screens row, place existing journeys to innovate or map out new ones.

Review existing journeys to explore how you can implement the solutions from the Digital Behaviour Solutions Canvas, and/or design new ones as needed.

Research existing journey solutions and add into the inspiration column for reference.

For all your digital solutions, refer to Sustainable Web Design strategies to design them in ways that minimise the energy they use.

Journey Solutions

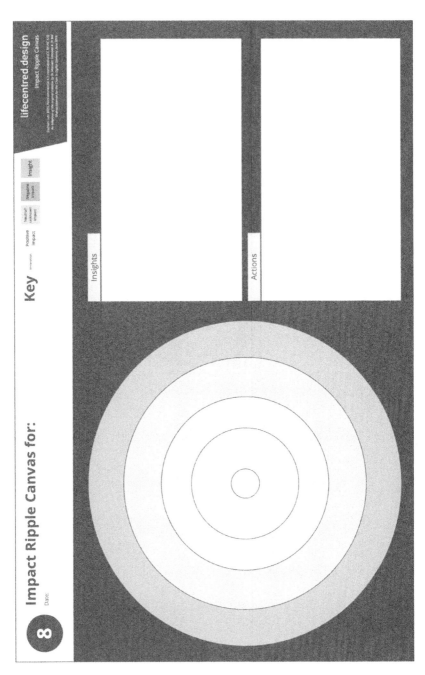

Figure 19 - Impact Ripple Canvas

8. Test from the futures

As you stroll by a river, with your new sense of presence and interconnectedness, the 'now' seems more vivid, alive, and playful.

You pick up a river pebble and throw it to skip it across the river's surface, each bounce causing ripples that glisten in the sunlight.

Your sense of interconnectedness, too, reaches out, to those who have lived before you, and to those yet to be born who will arrive in a world you leave for them.

Summary

Applying futures thinking, you'll aim to minimise unintended and potentially harmful consequences of your proposed innovations by speculating how their impacts might ripple out into the future.

Time: 10-30 mins

Method Tools: Impact Ripple Canvas

Design Modes: Speculating

Key steps:

1. Brainstorm impacts of your innovations
2. Analyse your ideas and summarise into key insights
3. Determine actions to address the insights

Expert Steps:

- Use participatory design
- Share with experts or a coalition for feedback

1. Brainstorm impacts of your innovations

The **Impact Ripple Canvas** was created by Dr Manuela Taboada & Dr Md Shahiduzzaman for exploring the unseen and unintended consequences of an action, decision, behaviour, trend, etc.

- Write your Persona's name in the centre circle of the canvas
- Write all your design innovations on stickies and place them in the first ripple around the Persona's name
- Brainstorm direct impacts of each innovation in the second ripple (and use a connecting line to show their connections)
- In the same ripple, brainstorm combined impacts of 2 or more innovations—use connecting lines again to show which innovations combine to cause the impact
- In the third ripple, repeat the method to brainstorm more indirect consequences of combined impacts
- Extend into new ripples of indirect and/or combined results as many times as desired
- Finish by brainstorming wider-reaching consequences by using the STEEPLE framework:

  o Society—How might human behaviours and societies change? How might minorities and the vulnerable be impacted?
  o Technology—What new technology might arise, or be abandoned, or how might they be used differently?
  o Environment—What greater environmental impact could this have?
  o Economic—How will spending habits change and what economies might be affected?
  o Politics—What power shifts may occur, and how might this affect freedoms, economies, etc?
  o Ethical—How will this change social responsibility in businesses, communities, and nations?

Example

Social media platforms collaborate with technology companies and a network of city councils and recycling facilities to make repair, collection, reuse, resell, and recycling the dominant behaviours, greatly reducing e-waste. However, the incomes of thousands of Ghanaians working in the dump sites—created by the e-waste sent to countries like Ghana—are destroyed. While this means these Ghanaians no longer must work in unsafe conditions, they had become to rely on the income to support themselves and their families.

2. Analyse your ideas and summarise into key insights

- Gather all the ideas into the *Insights* box
- Cluster them into themes
- Write a summary of each theme as a Key Insight
- Ask yourself, do any of these insights have the potential to hurt the non-human/non-user's needs, enable their threats, or hurt human needs?

3. Determine actions to address the insights

- In the *Actions* box, define any new actions or changes required to address the *Insights* and implement as needed

Ripple Canvas2

169

9. Summarise with a vision

Returning from your future thinking to the 'now', you craft a preferred future vision to retain the experience your journey has given you, so that it may ripple out to others and inspire a greater sense of presence and connection between all peoples, and between people and the land.

Summary

Compile all your refined innovations into a summary to communicate the vision to your team and beyond.

The process of creating a summary helps you synthesise your statements into one cohesive and regenerative solution.

As well as a usual summary document, look to produce a creative visual summary. Allow this artefact to become a little forward thinking to show your vision beyond what may be immediately viable, yet still realistic in the sense of what *could* be achieved in the near future with more dedicated life-centred action and funding. You can use the **Impact Ripple Canvas** to explore future impacts to 'futurise' the vision, and use AI 'text to image' tools to create visuals. For example:

- **Future web page**
- **Future Headlines**, fictional news headlines representing the positive impacts of your improved product or service on the world and your non-human/non-user
- **Before and After visuals**, of your lifecycle and/or non-human/non-user
- **Storyboard**, such as 'A Day in the Life" of your future users, non-humans/non-user
- **Short video**, such as a future commercial or documentary of your improved product or business
- **Social Media** stories, reels, or slideshows

10. Stay with them

Before you head back to your design studio, you gaze over the landscape one more time, seeing the world differently now as a living, breathing, interconnected flow of energy and life.

You understand and feel how everything you create must be a symbiotic part of the ecosystem, and that your creations come with a responsibility to ensure they remain so.

Summary

To fully shift from being just a sustainable producer to also being an ongoing regenerative caretaker, determine metrics to measure your innovations' impact on the non-humans/non-users. Embed them and your insights into your handover documents to ensure they are not forgotten or deprioritised after they leave your safe hands, and so you can monitor them in the future.

Time: NA

Method Tools: Any of your completed canvases and work that will help communicate the importance of the innovations, and create empathy in the team (e.g., your Personas, multi-media persona artefacts, Lifecycle Maps, Visual Summary, etc.)

Design Modes: Compiling, Sharing, and Monitoring

Key steps:

1. Determine metrics
2. Embed personas and their needs into handover documentation
3. Keep personas updated

Expert Steps:

- Explore forming an alliance between other organisations, from your industry and others, who share the same non-humans/non-users to create a library of ideas and to learn from and inspire each other
- Keep your experts/coalition involved by sharing with them any post-launch success and failures

1. Determine metrics

What would be the signs of success for your innovations and how can you measure and monitor them?

- What *existing* data could be used to measure the non-human/non-user's health, responses, behaviours, etc. related to your innovations?
- What *new* data could be used?
- How can you collect that data? What existing or new tech in your product/service can be used to capture and/or monitor data to give non-humans/non-users a voice?
- For animals interacting with your lifecycle, can you safely and ethically employ Animal-Computer Interaction systems that can also be used for tracking, such as:
  - Screen and Tracking Systems
  - Haptic and Wearable Systems
  - Tangible and Physical Systems
- Set up a cadence to check data post-launch and assess for impacts to the persona needs
- How will you hold yourself accountable for these solutions? For example, posting commitments on the website and updating progress/metrics

2. Embed non-humans/non-users and their needs in design handover

- Present the **Personas**, other **artefacts**, **Lifecycle Maps** and **Visual Summary** to the wider team, highlighting the design decisions made for the non-humans/non-users and the reasoning
- Embed **Personas**, metrics, etc. into design handover documentation
- Share multimedia persona artefacts to help business empathise more deeply
- Be available to answer any questions
- Allow others to edit and add to the personas as learnings arise

3. Keep personas updated

Update and evolve the personas over time:

- Update personas as learnings arise and each time you check post-launch
- Allow new primary personas to be discovered
- Know when to let personas go—for example if you created a persona for water and you managed to remove all use of water and any impacts to it, you wouldn't need to refer to water's needs anymore in design/decision-making (unless there was still healing to be done)

Other uses for non-human/non-user personas

Non-human/non-user personas can be used beyond the design process—get creative with how you can make the most of your research and keep non-human/non-user needs in wider conversations.

- Take to product feature demos, and all design, marketing and business decision-making sessions
- Share with colleagues, send personas out to business and ask How Might We? solve for their needs
- Put them on the walls with a QR code for more information (you can track these for engagement)
- Enable feedback to capture ideas and learn what's important to them
- Start embedding the use of non-human needs in the design and/or business decision-making process as a way of saying to business and actants 'We're not going to be human centred design, we're going to be life centred'
- Encourage business to use them beyond the design process, such as in marketing and in business decision meetings—make it easy for them by creating design principles
- Share with allies (e.g., Climate Designers, Client Earth, Earth Justice)
- Share principles and multi-media artefacts to inspire change in companies, customers, the general public, and governments
- Include in any futures envisioning

Part 5

-

Persona
Principles

Non-human/non-user Persona Principles

1. **A method and a tool**

   o   As a method, non-human/non-human personas are a process to learn, connect with and create empathy for nature, and create a shared understanding of a project's place in nature and its impacts

   o   As a tool, non-human/non-human personas summarise needs and key considerations for including them in design and business decisions

2. **Data-based and unbiased**

   o   Be data-based and wary of stereotypes—Stay vigilant against gathering information that is purely opinion-based, stereotyping, and/or wishful thinking

3. **Multi-format**

   o   Initially, and at minimum, create a main persona for each non-human/non-user as a source of truth which can then be translated into other artefacts of different mediums, such as video, audio, etc., as needed

4. **To be shared**

   o   If at times participatory design can't be employed, keep business and impacted parties involved by sharing with them the key stages of the persona process

5. **Apply to all channels**

   o   Websites
   o   Apps
   o   Newsletters and communications
   o   Marketing strategies and services, etc.

6. **Expect trade-offs**

   o   Just as there are trade-offs between the user and business needs, there will also be trade-offs when prioritising design decisions between life-centred thinking and human-centred thinking as the world transitions to a less human-centred paradigm

7. **Persona work is dynamic**

   o Identifying and defining personas can be iterative throughout the process:

     ▪ Be open to discovering new non-human/non-users throughout the process and pivoting to focus on them if needed
     ▪ Ensure the personas are updated and grow over time, as the designer and business learn more about the non-humans/non-users
     ▪ Manually check for updates to data you've included, constantly explore metrics and ways to test, and update personas as learnings arise
     ▪ Know when to let personas go—for example if you created a persona for water and you managed to remove all use of water and any impacts to it, you wouldn't need to refer water's needs anymore in design/decision-making (unless there is healing still to be done)

8. **Multi-purpose**

   o Non-human/non-user personas and artefacts can be used beyond the design process:

     ▪ Vary persona formats—Use personas to influence by sharing them with the team and business and including them in their creation — try multi-media formats such as audio and video files for engaging actants and the public
     ▪ Create future visions of your product or service
     ▪ Influence and inspire other organisations to change
     ▪ Communicate and create public awareness of non-human/non-user
     ▪ Collaborate with allies

9. **For new and existing projects**

   o Use non-human personas to be used throughout the design process and referred to as often as human user personas, and use them to retrospectively assess and innovate existing designs

10. Be mindful of limitations

- o Non-human/non-user personas can have the same limitations as human personas, such as lack of accuracy and completeness, being made with biased images and content and harmful stereotyping, generalisation leaving out the marginalised, and not being updated or referred to often enough (weakening empathy)—and these can cause unintended rebound effects
- o The effects of using personas may take a long time to manifest and measure, as regeneration projects such as new forests take years to grow and show their positive impact.

Part 6

–

Looking back
to look ahead

You walk into your spacious, brightly lit studio with your design team and gather around a large table adorned with sketches, prototypes, and samples of various wood.

A soft humming permeates the room, and a shimmering hologram materializes in the centre of the table—a magnificent tree.

The hologram emanates a soothing, ethereal glow, and its branches gracefully sway. Made of thousands of smaller trees, it is a digital twin representing all forests. The hologram facilitates communication between the designers and the local trees using a newly developed interspecies communication technology.

The leaves shimmer as if touched by a gentle breeze and a melodic voice resonates through the room to greet you and your team.

You share prototypes of your product with the digital twin for guidance on how the design might impact the local trees and their supporting lifeforms.

In response, the tree speaks of the interconnectedness of its own design, how every part of it works harmoniously to fulfill its purpose in nature, how its branches play a unique role in supporting life, filtering air and soil, and conserving energy, how the trunk's structure provides strength and stability while using minimal resources, and how its roots absorb nutrients efficiently from the soil.

You discuss with your team how you can further incorporate these principles into your design, seeking to emulate the efficiency and resilience found in the tree's natural architecture.

The tree further highlights its pollution-free features, how its leaves serve as natural air filters, purifying the surrounding environment. Leaves, depicted as intricate patterns of interconnected cells, also show you how they transform sunlight into energy through photosynthesis.

Inspired by this, your team envision integrating air purification technology within your design, allowing it to contribute to cleaner indoor spaces, and incorporating solar cells, allowing it to harness renewable energy for various purposes.

You ask your digital muse how to better work with local businesses and communities, and the hologram showcases how trees collaborate with other organisms, sharing resources and nurturing one another, ultimately forming a harmonious ecosystem.

As the hologram continues to share its insights, you and your team form a symbiotic relationship with the local trees, facilitated by the holographic digital twin, merging human ingenuity with nature's wisdom, exchanging ideas, and sketching concepts, transcending traditional design boundaries, and embracing a future where the environment and innovation intertwine seamlessly.

Driven by a newfound sense of purpose, your team embarks on a design journey that harmonizes both aesthetics and environmental consciousness, drawing inspiration from the interconnectedness and sustainable design principle. You develop ways to promote forest regeneration, such as supporting tree-planting initiatives, partnering with organizations that protect and restore forests, and embedding your product with seeds so when it becomes unrepairable it can be replanted to reproduce many more forests.

***

In futuring design practices—such as speculative design, design fiction, and foresight—futurists study news and behaviours to find signals of changes that might grow, become trends, and alter the projected future such as the signals in this story—interspecies communication, holographs, digital twins, and designers collaborating with nature.

Futurists mix these signals to generate potential future scenarios to open our mind to what's possible.

But to look ahead, we must also look to the past to understand how we got here. Sometimes, there are signals of the past re-emerging in the future, re-appreciated and newly integrated.

If we look to the past of how humans connected with other species, we might find the most profound and effective evolution of non-human personas.

Totems

As mentioned in the introductory chapter, non-human personas are related to a much older concept connecting humans to animals and nature—the First Nations use of totems to represent non-human entities like natural objects, plants, animals, spirit beings, or even the weather.

Different cultures use different terms, for example:

- *Auguds*, from Torres Strait Islanders
- *Jadiny*, from Australian Aboriginals

How totems are identified (and how many), how they are connected to a person or group, and how they are used, all differ between cultures, and even between groups within cultures.

Examples of relationships with totems:

- As guides and lesson teachers
- To represent certain attributes or values for personal growth—For example, in Indigenous North American totemism, an alligator represents stealth and a fight for survival, while the ant represents teamwork and overall perseverance
- To identify the different responsibilities of each clan
- To represent non-human beings to be respected, nurtured, protected, and knowledge about them shared and preserved

Examples of how totems are gained:

- Chosen by an Elder or family member, and given at a young age or Coming of Age Ceremony
- Self-chosen, which can be therapeutic and spiritual or a more practical choice for personal growth
- The totem 'chooses the person', via ceremony or identified in key moments in one's life

Examples of the number of totems per person/clan:

- In Indigenous Australian totemism, each person can have four totems, one each for the nation, clan, family, and an individual totem
- The Ojibwe peoples use one totem per clan

While there are many variations of totemism, there is also a common underlying purpose, which is to consider the world beyond humans—and to consider these things not just as resources but as lifeforms to be respected, by forming relationships and a sense of responsibility between humans and the natural world, which directly correlates with the purpose of non-human personas.

So how might we evolve the use of non-human personas in the design and business world by learning from the traditional and ecological wisdom of totemism?

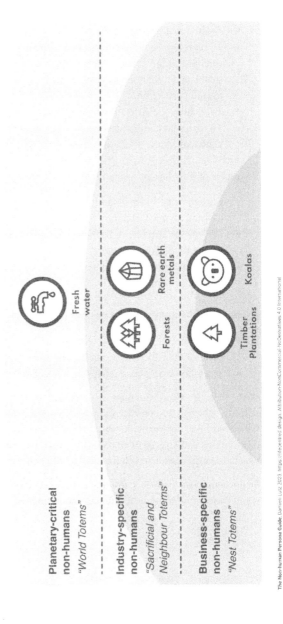

The non-human totems of a small business

The non-humans for a website selling digital and paperback books, represented by totems

Planetary-critical non-humans
"World Totems"

Fresh water

Industry-specific non-humans
"Sacrificial and Neighbour Totems"

Forests

Rare earth metals

Business-specific non-humans
"Nest Totems"

Timber Plantations

Koalas

The Non-human Persona Guide. Damien Lutz 2023. https://interpreted design. Attribution-NonCommercial-NoDerivatives 4.0 International

Figure 20 - Totems of a small business

Determining the totems of a product or business

Products and businesses could determine their totems according to their common resources by taking inspiration from how totems are traditionally determined:

- Determined by 'family member'—This could correlate to the industry that the product/business belongs to ('Industry Totems'). For example, any printer of paper goods could automatically gain a 'Trees and Forests' totem. Any business selling personal devices could automatically gain 'Rare earth metals' and 'E-waste' as totems. Perhaps these Industry Totems could also be defined by two types of relationships, those non-humans directly sacrificed as resources (Sacrificial Totems), and those indirectly impacted by the lifecycle (Neighbour Totems).
- Determined by 'self'—Each individual product or business could also determine their own totems to represent any non-humans their specific business impacts beyond the industry commons (let's call these 'Nest Totems' for now)
- Thinking globally, and taking inspiration from modern science, perhaps all businesses could also gain at least one global totem to represent non-humans in urgent danger worldwide (World Totems). They might be a species near extinction or the most threatened planetary ecosystems

Using words like 'Sacrificial', 'Neighbour', 'Nest', and 'World' rather than 'resource', 'ecosystem', and 'global' might connect us more deeply to the lifeforms we are taking from and/or damaging.

A small business and its totems

As an example subject, let's use a website that sells digital and paperback books (see Figure 20).

Based on two key industries this business belongs to (the book publishing industry and tech industry), it could automatically belong to the following Sacrificial Totems:

- Coniferous Trees & Forests (Book publishing industry)
- Rare Earth metals and E-Waste (Digital tech industry)

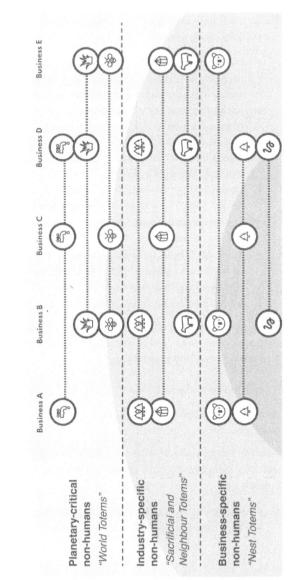

Figure 21 - Businesses with common totems

And the business would then automatically belong to the Neighbour Totems to represent the ecosystems impacted by the business supply chain and lifecycle. As an example:

- Village ecosystems damaged by rare earth metal mining and factories used for the technology needed for the business' website and for the e-readers required to enjoy its books

The business might also identify Nest Totems, based on the specifics of its business, such as its locality:

- Timber plantations in NSW (if we determined the paper for the printed books came from NSW)
- Koala or other animals impacted by timber plantations

Our hypothetical business would also belong to a World Totem, such as:

- Clean water (To connect to all the water used in paper and technology production and their contribution to the worsening water scarcity)

Employing non-human personas as totems

All businesses might then be 'related' by their totems and collaborate to care for them, whether they are competing in the same industry or from different industries, creating networks that transcend traditional barriers of collaboration.

Since these totems would be used by so many, their personas could be a collective knowledge, meaning individual groups, organisations, and businesses would create, evolve, and maintain the personas collaboratively, with the added benefits of reducing inaccuracy and sharing strategies.

Drawing from their collective knowledge and guided by the traditional wisdom of totemism, collaborating businesses could use their prosperity, innovation, and influence to develop ways to:

- Replace or reduce the use of their Sacrificial Totems
- Reduce and restore the impact on their Neighbour Totems
- Enrich healthy instances of their Sacrificial and Neighbour Totems
- Learn about their totems and teach others and the public about them
- Understand the specific characteristics of their totems (strength, community, perseverance, etc.) and champion these values in themselves and in others

As the developed world with its human-centred design sees itself 'evolving' into a more life-centred iteration, with tools such as non-human and non-user personas, it is really just remembering what First Nations people recognised tens of thousands of years ago—humans need to respect and nurture the two most important relationships, that between people and people, and that between people and land.

***

If you enjoyed this guide and its resources, please leave a review on the site where you made the purchase. Reviews help self-funded books like this one get found and read.

More books by the author

The Life-centred Design Guide

lifecentred.design

Life-centred design expands human-centred design to include consideration for the planet and all life forms by aligning designers with global goals.

Life-centred design is still emerging, however, so awareness of it is low, those who practise it are few, how it is practised varies, and hybridisation of physical and digital product design strategies is nascent.

The Life-Centred Design Guide introduces a collection of today's life-centred design approaches and speculates a 'Future Snapshot' of what the framework might become if the variations merged, complete with downloadable tools to start experimenting.

Future Scouting

futurescouting.com.au

Future Scouting is a fun and practical step-by-step guide to designing fantastic and thought-provoking design fiction prototypes to inspire better tomorrows—an exciting practice known as speculative design.

The book includes downloadable tools to:

- Catch a signal of emerging change
- Design a future invention
- Ideate a key scenario
- Extrude a Hero and future world
- Compile your artefacts into a shareable prototype

Keep this book circular

As a responsible prosumer, you now steward the natural resources of this book. Here's a few tips on how to keep it circular.

Maintain and repair

See *wikihow.com/Repair-a-Paperback-Book* for ways to:

- Clean the book
- Repair loose and torn pages
- Reattach a cover
- Fix the binding

Just make sure you use an *environmentally friendly craft glue*, ones with low VOC (volatile organic compounds), are petrochemical free, and/or water-based.

Don't want to keep it anymore?

Pass the book on to someone who can use it:
- A friend
- A school
- Drop it in at a local library
- Pop it in a street library box

Can't give it away?

Paperbacks can generally be recycled, so check your local rules to make sure you can drop it in the paper recycling bin.

Acknowledgements

The Non-Human Persona Guide draws on the great work of sustainable, regenerative, and socially just practitioners, thinkers, and innovators who have in various ways expanded the idea of what design should be. I'm very thankful for the inspiration their work has given me, and I hope this book flows that inspiration forward to many others.

Special thanks to those who have generously shared their insights from experimenting with non-human personas— Monika Sznel, Martin Tomitsch, Victor Udoewa, Sandy Daehnert, Jeroen Spoelstra, Fiona Tout, and Ben Serbutt.

I also acknowledge the Gadigal people of the Eora Nation and Elders as the Traditional Custodians of the Country where I live and work. I recognise their continuing connection to the land and waters and thank them for continuing to share their knowledge and ways of being.

About the author

Damien Lutz is a UX Designer and writer in Sydney, Australia.

He is the author of three design guides—Future Scouting, The Life-centred Design Guide, The Non-Human Persona Guide, and he created their respective online learning hubs, futurescouring.com.au and lifecentred.design.

In 2021, he co-founded The Life-centred Design Collective and shares his life-centred and futuring projects and insights on his Medium blog.

Damien is also the author three science fiction books—Amanojaku, The Lenz, and Ten Past Now.

Printed in Great Britain
by Amazon

39351946R00118